THE WORLD WAR 1 TRIVIA BOOK

Interesting Stories and Random Facts from the First World War

BY
BILL O'NEILL

DON'T FORGET YOUR
FREE BOOKS

GET THEM FOR FREE ON
WWW.TRIVIABILL.COM

CONTENTS

INTRODUCTION..1

CHAPTER ONE: THE CAUSES OF THE WAR..........5

Flying the Flag: The Emergence of
Nationalism in Western Europe...............................6

The Problem of the Austro-Hungarian
Empire...8

The Colonial Rush for Africa...................................10

Carving Up Asia...12

The Sick Man of Europe..12

"Don't Tread on Me!"...14

The Empire the Sun Never Sat On 16

Russia and the "Great Game" 17

The Alliance System: The Central Powers.............19

Great Britain and the Triple Entente 22

Lingering Resentments 23

Russia Needs Some Friends......................................24

A Doomed Archduke...25

The Straw that Broke the Camel's Back 27

War is Declared 28

Random Facts..30

Test Yourself – Questions and Answers..........................35

　　Answers 36

CHAPTER TWO: THE EARLY WAR 37

　　The Schlieffen Plan...37

　　Kinks in the Plan...39

　　The First Battle of the Marne – September 6-10, 1914...40

　　A Family Affair 41

　　Why Did the Germans Wear Those Pointed Helmets?..42

　　The Eastern Front...44

　　The War in Africa..46

　　The War in the Middle East.................................47

　　The Gallipoli Campaign 48

　　Lawrence of Arabia..49

　　The Armenian Genocide 51

　　Why Trench Warfare?..52

　　Living, Fighting, and Dying in the Trenches.........55

　　The Battle of the Somme....................................56

　　Hitler in the Trenches 56

　Random Facts 59

　Test Yourself – Questions and Answers..........................63

　　Answers 64

CHAPTER THREE: THE WAR DRAGS ON 65

    Here Come the Tanks! 66

    Air Recon...67

    Death From Above...................................69

    The Red Baron 70

    Not the Goodyear Blimp.........................71

    Dreadnoughts and the British Navy 73

    U-Boat Warfare......................................74

    U-151 75

    A Chance for Peace?...............................76

    The Italian Front....................................77

    Who Remained Neutral in Europe?......78

    The Concept of Chemical Warfare 79

    The Second Battle of Ypres 80

    Using Chemical Weapons.......................81

    The Horrors of Chemical Warfare..........82

Random Facts..84

Test Yourself – Questions and Answers...........88

    Answers 89

CHAPTER FOUR: INTERMISSION, THE
BOLSHEVIK REVOLUTION 90

    The Romanov Dynasty 91

    Das Kapital 92

A Detached Monarchy.................................... 95

Lenin, Trotsky, and the Boys........................ 96

The Russo-Japanese War 97

The 1905 Revolution 99

Nicky and His Family.................................. 100

Russia Enters the War................................. 101

The February Revolution............................. 102

The Bolshevik Revolution 104

Brest-Litovsk 105

The Murder of the Romanovs 106

Russia Forgotten?.. 107

Civil War 108

A New Economic Policy.............................. 109

Random Facts 111

Test Yourself – Questions and Answers......... 116

Answers 117

CHAPTER FIVE: THE AMERICANS ENTER
THE WAR.. 118

A Rural America 119

German-Americans..................................... 121

Irish-Americans... 122

The Socialists.. 123

Americans Who Favored War.................................124

The Evil Hun 125

The Sinking of the Lusitania.............................128

The Zimmerman Telegram...............................129

The Homefront after War Was Declared 130

The Espionage Act and the Sedition Act 132

The Selective Service Act 133

Here Come the Doughboys! 134

Fighting the Germans and the Spanish Flu 136

General "Black Jack" Pershing 138

The Hundred Days Offensive 140

Random Facts...141

Test Yourself – Questions and Answers.....................145

Answers 147

CHAPTER SIX: THE PEACE AND
UNRESOLVED ISSUES FROM THE WAR.............148

To the Victors Go the Spoils 149

The Treaty of Versailles 151

Problems with Versailles 152

The Fate of Austria-Hungary 153

The Fate of the Ottoman Empire.........................154

The League of Nations...156

The Balfour Declaration 157

Veterans Day 158

Shell Shock 160

The Bonus Army 161

All Quiet on the Western Front 163

Ernst Jünger 164

Frank Buckles 165

Post Script: The Balkans War 166

How Do We Study World War One? 167

Random Facts 169

Test Yourself – Questions and Answers 174

Answers 176

MORE BOOKS BY BILL O'NEILL 179

INTRODUCTION

You probably know a few things about World War Two, but what do you know about World War One?

Let's face it, in terms of media coverage World War Two gets all the glory and therefore many people know very little about World War One. In addition, educators spend far more time on World War Two than they do on World War One.

Of course, there are many reasons for this: far more people died in World War Two, the ending of World War Two led into the Cold War, and there are still some living survivors of World War Two. With that said, World War One was almost as, if not just as important as World War Two.

And if you think about it, you probably know more than a few things about World War One.

You probably know that the assassination of a European leader set off the war, although you may not be sure who that person was. I bet you know that the United States, Great Britain, Russia, and France were on one side and Germany was on the other. But you probably have to think for a while who Germany's allies were and might be surprised that one of them was the Ottoman Empire.

You may even know a little bit about the German ace pilot, the Red Baron.

But have you ever considered the events that led up to World War One? Why did the field commanders think trench warfare was a good idea? How did air warfare and sea warfare play a role in the war? What was the purpose of chemical warfare? How did the United States get involved and what impact did it have? What role did the rise of communism play in World War One? What were the final results of the war?

All of these questions and more are answered in the following book in a lively manner that will at times put you right in the trenches next to the soldiers. This book will bring what was once known as the "Great War" and the "War to End All Wars" to life in a way that few other historians of World War One have done.

Although this book follows a general chronology of World War One, it focuses on themes and topics that are not only historically important, but also interesting for you the reader in the twenty-first century. Yes, World War One ended just over 100 years ago but its impact continues to be felt today around the world in many ways.

World War One lasted just over four years, but the events and ideas that led to it began during the middle of the eighteenth century and many of its impacts are still being felt today, especially in southeastern Europe. Although the war itself is the focus of this book, a 100 plus year timeline will be covered.

Ultimately the point of this book is to educate you the reader about World War One in a way that is entertaining and fun.

It's broken up into six easy chapters, each with fifteen stories about the chapter's main topic. They'll introduce you to the most important events and people in the war in an interesting way. They'll also help you understand the hard facts and the politics well enough to discuss them at your next dinner party or history class. Each chapter also comes with a whole section full of quick, surprising facts to wow your friends and a few challenging trivia questions to test your knowledge.

Some of the things you learn in this book will be scary, perplexing, and even bizarre, but they are all true.

So get ready to find out…

How did communism play an important role in the war?

Why were Americans were divided on entering the war?

What did Hitler do during the war and what happened to his dog?

How were all the royal families on both sides of the war connected?

And much, much more.

CHAPTER ONE

THE CAUSES OF THE WAR

World War One began when the now non-existent nation-state of Austria-Hungary declared war on the tiny country of Serbia in 1914. Over the next four years, the world was thrust into what many thought was going to be the final war in history.

And there were several reasons why people thought that.

Over nine million combatants died during the war along with more than seven million civilians, making it the costliest war up until that time in terms of human lives and physical damage to property. Major battles were fought on three continents and the waters of the North Atlantic Ocean were unsafe for travel, even for civilians, for most of the war. But World War One didn't just happen overnight. There were a number of factors that contributed to the war, some of which began decades earlier during the nineteenth century. Keep reading to find out what were some of the major factors that led to the Great War.

Flying the Flag: The Emergence of Nationalism in Western Europe

In order to understand the origins of World War One, we have to discuss the concept of *nationalism* and in order to do that we have to go back to the period in the 1700s known as the Enlightenment.

The Enlightenment took place all throughout western Europe, but it was mainly centered in Great Britain, France, and Germany kingdoms. It was a period of high philosophy, where people questioned many things and advocated modern ideas of republican and democratic governments to replace the ancient monarchies.

The Enlightenment influenced the American and French revolutions and a little French military commander you may have heard of – Napoleon Bonaparte.

When Napoleon tore through Europe like a lightning bolt during the Napoleonic Wars (1803-1815), he often dismantled the old monarchies of his conquests in favor of new democratic-republican type governments.

Of course Napoleon only did so to create governments that were sympathetic and loyal to him, but his actions planted the first seeds of nationalism. With the monarchies either gone or severely diminished in power, the various European peoples looked for something new to rally around.

The answer for many was nationalism.

Since there was no single guide book of nationalism ever written—no "nationalism for dummies" if you will—and nationalism meant different things to different people, its definition can be a bit fluid. Simply put, nationalism is pride in one's background. In terms of western Europe in the nineteenth century and how it influenced the start of World War One, the specific concept of "political nationalism" is what we need to consider.

Political nationalism, as it was thought of and practiced in Europe in the nineteenth century, was the idea that all people of one nationality should be unified in one nation-state.

In other words, all Germans should be in an all-German nation-state, all Italians should be in an all-Italian nation-state etc.

This may seem self-evident today when you consider the modern borders of Europe, but this was not so for most of European history. In the medieval and even early modern periods of European history the continent was divided into kingdoms where the subjects of a king may speak several different languages. For example, the king of England held lands in France into the early modern period.

This began to change in the years after the Napoleonic Wars.

Europeans began to identify more with their neighbors than their kings and the idea of creating new nation-states caught steam by the middle of the century.

Germany achieved almost total unification on January 18, 1871 after the Franco-Prussian War and Italy also achieved unification that same year, which they called the *Risorgimento*.

Once the larger European nationalities achieved unification, the smaller nationalities tried to follow in their footsteps.

The Problem of the Austro-Hungarian Empire

As far as nationalism was concerned, perhaps the biggest elephant in the room before World War One was the Austro-Hungarian Empire.

To put it frankly, the Austro-Hungarian Empire was a hot mess.

It was a tinderbox waiting to explode and a relic of Europe's medieval past, but it was also a powerful country located in the middle of the continent. As the name of the country implies, the Austro-Hungarian Empire, or simply Austria-Hungary, was a country that formed in 1867 when the royal families of Austria and Hungary united. At a time when most western Europeans were moving toward ethnically homogenous nation-states, the Austro-Hungarian

Empire seemingly went in the opposite direction.

The elite class of Austria-Hungary was comprised of ethnic Germans (Austrians) and Magyars (Hungarians), which caused some confusion and consternation among the upper class, but the true problems came from the great mass of the empire's subjects.

Most of the subjects of the Austro-Hungarian Empire were ethnic Slavs: Serbs, Croats, Slovenes, Slovaks, and Czechs.

Many Romanians also lived within the confines of the kingdom, as well as a fair amount of Ukrainians, Poles, and Italians.

As nationalism took hold of western Europe in the early and mid-nineteenth century, a very specific eastern European form, known as "Pan-Slavism," became popular later in the century. Some Pan-Slavic philosophers believed that all Slavic people should be under one single nation-state, while other more pragmatic thinkers simply believed that Slavs should have their own countries. The Russian Empire was one of the major proponents of the philosophy, which would play a role in the events directly leading to the start of World War 1.

Pan-Slavism also played a role in the more recent Balkans Wars, which will be discussed later in this book.

The Colonial Rush for Africa

By the early twentieth century the major Western powers controlled most of the non-Western world. Great Britain, France, Germany, Russia, and even the United States combined to control the majority of the planet's landmass, but the British held the most colonies by far.

But we'll get to them in a minute.

Of course, the reason for this control was the control of resources such as spices, gold, silver, diamonds, and tobacco, and later oil and other Industrial Age resources. The scramble for these resources sometimes ended with the European powers fighting each other, but also sometimes in a strange type of cooperation as was the case in China during the nineteenth century when they agreed to terms of control on "treaty ports." The treaty ports were simply Chinese port cities that the major powers controlled, sometimes jointly.

The age of European imperialism and colonialism began in the sixteenth century when Spanish and Portuguese explorers surveyed the African coast, which was soon followed by expeditions of conquest. By the middle of the nineteenth century nearly all of Africa, with the exceptions of Liberia and Ethiopia, were controlled directly by European powers. Great Britain and France claimed the most African colonies, but Spain, Portugal, and Germany also had smaller colonies on the continent.

The gold and diamonds the British received from their African colonies was highly coveted by the others, especially the Germans.

You probably don't think of Germany as having a major historical influence in Africa. After all, English is the most widely spoken language on the continent, but in the nineteenth and early twentieth centuries the Germans also had considerable African colonies. Germany had the colonies of Togoland (the modern countries of Cameroon and Ghana), German East Africa (Burundi, Rwanda, and Tanzania), and German Southwest Africa (Namibia).

The problem was that most of the German-African colonies were lacking in resources and were surrounded by the British. German politicians believed that in order to accommodate their growing population they either had to increase their borders in Europe or they had to increase their colonial holdings to produce more resources.

Those who favored the second option wanted to focus their attention on Africa, with the possibility of gaining new colonies.

South Africa was always in the minds of German politicians and military leaders: it's vast resources, a modern infrastructure, and a large white population that was inherently hostile toward the British.

Keep this in mind as we move on.

Carving Up Asia

In many ways, the colonial situation in Asia was similar to Africa. Although the people in Asia were different than those in Africa, the primary colonial powers were Britain and France. As mentioned earlier, the treaty port situation opened things up a bit for other potential colonial powers, though. Even non-traditional colonial powers such as the United States, Russia, and Japan had some troops in Chinese ports.

Germany and the Austro-Hungarian Empire also had troops in some Chinese ports, but all of that began coming to an end when China experienced its own authentic version of nationalism. The Boxer Rebellion (1899-1901), so named by Western soldiers because the Chinese fighters were adherents in martial arts, marked the beginning of the end of the treaty port system.

Although the Western powers put down the rebellion, most realized that China could no longer be controlled by foreign guns.

Germany and Austria-Hungary would have to look elsewhere to accommodate the growth of their nations.

The Sick Man of Europe

If you'd told an ethnic Turk in the sixteenth century that in three hundred years his country would be called the "sick man of Europe," he would've probably laughed at you, or cut off your head.

During the sixteenth century, the Ottoman Empire was not only the largest and most powerful Islamic dynasty of the period—and some historians today would argue it was the third great caliphate—but it was also firmly involved in the affairs of Europe. The Ottoman Turks controlled a large part of southeastern Europe, as well as most of North Africa and the Islamic holy sites of Mecca and Medina.

The Ottomans also controlled the overland routes that connected Asia and Europe, which helped to make them into an economic as well as a military powerhouse.

But when it comes to love, war, and empires, things can quickly change.

The discovery and subsequent colonization of the New World by the European powers and technological discoveries made in Europe, combined with a general cultural apathy among the Turks, meant that the Ottoman Turks were quickly being eclipsed by their European neighbors.

By the eighteenth century the Ottomans ceased to be a major player in western Europe and by the nineteenth century the Russians were taking what they had left in the Crimea region of the Black Sea.

The term "sick man of Europe" is actually credited to Nicholas I of Russia (ruled 1825-1855), who described the Ottoman Empire as such during the Crimean War (1853-1856).

To make matters worse, the ever expansive and vibrant British Empire turned a covetous eye toward the petroleum-rich region of Mesopotamia (Iraq), which was controlled by the Ottomans. The Ottoman sultans of the late nineteenth century knew that their kingdom was on its last legs unless they made some drastic moves. They began forging closer military and economic ties with Germany with the intention of at least keeping all of their imperial possessions, if not expanding them.

If war were to break out with Britain, the Ottoman leaders reasoned, perhaps they could recapture and some of their former possessions in the Middle East, such as Egypt.

Perhaps it was too much to ask of the Sick Man Europe, but in the age of empires anything was possible.

"Don't Tread on Me!'

You might be wondering, "If the Germans, Austrian-Hungarians, and Ottomans wanted to expand their empires but couldn't in Asia and Africa without fighting the other major powers, why didn't they just invade Latin America?" The question makes sense. Most Latin American countries were too small, poor, and technologically behind the major powers to put up a reasonable fight and there were/are considerable resources in Latin America to be exploited. But the reason why that never happened came down to one simple concept . . .

The Monroe Doctrine.

You may remember reading about the Monroe Doctrine way back in high school, but if you didn't, here's a quick recap and how it related to the start of World War 1.

American President James Monroe (in office 1817-1825) announced the doctrine during his State of the Union address in 1825. Essentially, he stated that if any of the European powers interfered with the governments of the newly independent Latin American countries, the United States would intervene. It was not actually called the "Monroe Doctrine" until 1850 and for several decades most of Europe never took the doctrine very seriously.

To them, the United States was never a threat, but most of those countries also had no interests in Latin America.

That changed during the Spanish-American War of 1898.

During that war, Cubans revolted against Spanish rule and were supported by the United States, which really for the first time attempted to enforce the Monroe Doctrine. The result was an overwhelming victory for the United States, the affirmation of the Monroe Doctrine, and the U.S.'s official entry into the imperial club as it gained Puerto Rico, Guam, and the Philippines as colonies.

So the Monroe Doctrine effectively kept the European colonial powers out of Latin America during the period of modern empires.

The Empire the Sun Never Sat On

You've probably heard the phrase "the Empire the Sun Never Sat On" at some point in your life, but do you know what it means or how it relates to World War One? It was a term that referred to the British Empire at its height in the late nineteenth century. During that time, the British controlled a quarter of the Earth's surface, had colonies on every continent, and had the most diverse range of subject population than any other empire.

In order to understand why the British built such an expansive empire and how it related to World War One, you need to understand that England, Wales, and Scotland are collectively an island that is about the same size as the state of Tennessee, but with a much larger population.

In order for the British population to grow and for their government and economy to prosper, they needed to either acquire more land in Europe or conquer territories on other continents, which would be the "colonial model."

The British obviously chose the colonial model, which limited the other European powers' ability to follow suite without coming into conflict with them. When the king of Germany, called the "Kaiser," Wilhelm II (ruled 1888-1918), publicly announced that his country was going to pursue the same imperial policy as Britain, it put the British on high alert.

By the year 1900, it appeared to many that Germany and Great Britain were bound to come to blows over colonialism.

Russia and the "Great Game"

Russia is a strange and fascinating country. The western part of Russia, where most of its people live, is located in Europe, but most of its landmass is in Asia. Besides the ethnic Russians who make up the majority of the population, Russia has been the home to many different central Asian nationalities, including: Armenians, Chechens, Azerbaijanis, Kazaks, and numerous other Mongol descended peoples.

Russia has also traditionally had Muslim and Buddhist minorities.

And although the Russian people are Christian by tradition, they are Orthodox Christians, which is a different form of Christianity than that practiced in the West. The cultural differences between Russia and western Europe led many eminent historians, such as Arnold Toynbee, to declare that Russia was part of an Orthodox Christian Civilization, which although related to the West was certainly distinct.

Throughout history, the Russian people have both celebrated and fought against their differences from their western European neighbors. Russian Tsar Peter I "the Great" (ruled 1682-1725) imported western European scientists and philosophers to not only modernize Russian in terms of technology, but also to Westernize the country's culture. Catherine II "the Great" (ruled 1762-1796), who was actually an ethnic German raised in a German kingdom, followed suite.

Still, Russia lagged behind the Western powers in terms of technology, economy, and prestige, so by the nineteenth century the tsars decided to enter into the colonial competition.

Although the Russians faced the same dilemma as the Germans and Austrian-Hungarians as far as there being a lack of colonies to capture in Africa and Asia, they had the advantage of a large landmass that bordered central and eastern Asia.

The Russians would simply move across their

southern border into places like Persia, Mongolia, and central Asia to satisfy their imperial aims.

So began the period known as the "Great Game."

The Great Game was played between Russia, which was gobbling up central Asian kingdoms throughout the nineteenth century, and Britain, which was of course the premier colonial power at the time. The Ottoman Empire was the biggest loser during the Great Game, but the British felt threatened enough to check Russian expansionism during the Crimean War.

The Japanese then bloodied the Russian bear's nose in the Russo-Japanese War of 1905, temporarily halting Russian expansion in East Asia.

Although the Russians may have lost to the Japanese, they were at that point established as a colonial and military power.

Whether the western Europeans liked it or not, Russia would be involved in any major events during the twentieth century.

The Alliance System: The Central Powers

You may think it's strange that along with the rise of nationalism and colonialism, most historians attribute the early twentieth century alliance structure as one of the primary causes of World War One. After all, aren't alliances supposed to stop wars?

When you think about the Cold War alliance system of NATO and the Warsaw Pact, it does seem like the existence of those alliances may have prevented World War Three—strength deterred strength.

Mutually assured destruction and all that.

But things were much different in the early twentieth century. There were no nuclear weapons and, remember, there had not yet been a total "world" war.

For all intents and purposes, the world was in uncharted territory when it came to this new type of war.

The World War One alliance system worked like any alliance before or after it in history. If one member was attacked then it was the responsibility of all the other members to join the fray. It was quite simple but no one anticipated that in 1914 the alliance system would lead to a geopolitical gang war.

On one side was the Central Powers alliance, so-called because the original member nations—Germany, Austria-Hungary, and Italy—were all located in central Europe. This original alliance of Germany, Austria-Hungary, and Italy was known as the Triple Alliance of 1882 and it became the forerunner of the later Central Powers Alliance. The Ottoman Empire joined the Central Powers after the war began, in August 1914, as did Bulgaria in October 1915. The goals of Germany, Austria-Hungary, and the Ottoman Empire have already been discussed in terms of nationalism and imperial aspirations, but what was the small country of Bulgaria thinking by getting involved in the alliance?

Although Bulgaria was small, it too had some territorial ambitions. It hoped to gain back territories it had lost in previous wars to Romania, Greece, and Serbia and thought that joining the Central Powers would be its best path to achieve that goal.

Everything then makes sense, right? But what about Italy?

Shortly after World War One began, Italy switched sides. Italy has been the butt of jokes over this move, but really its behavior was not much different than any other country at the time. Italy had its own imperial ambitions, so when the war began it officially stayed neutral, arguing that the alliance it signed with Germany and Austria-Hungary in 1882 was purely defensive.

Then the British and French gave them an offer they couldn't refuse.

The Italians were offered to keep land they took from Austria-Hungary on their northern border if they joined the fight against their former allies. It was an offer they couldn't refuse, so in 1915 they declared war on the Central Powers and opened up a third European front in the war.

Still, even without the Italians, the Central Powers was a strong alliance.

Great Britain and the Triple Entente

In opposition to the Central Powers alliance was the alliance known as the Triple Entente, which is French for friendship. The alliance was signed on August 31, 1907 between Great Britain, France, and Russia.

You might not know this, but Japan was actually added to the alliance later and of course the United States.

But that was much later, at least in terms of where we are at now in our story.

If you were an average Englishman living in London in 1907, drinking your tea and ale and eating your blood pudding, you may've thought this was an extremely strange agreement. After all, it was not long before this that your grandfather fought the Russians in the Crimea and his father fought Napoleon's forces at Waterloo.

But as an Englishman you'd also be a very practical person and would've realized that geopolitics and international alliances are more practical than they are personal. By the early twentieth century the "Great Game" with Russia was all but over and the rivalry with France was a thing of the past. To the British, the Germans were the primary threat to their empire, whether that be in Africa or on the European continent.

For the British, their membership in the Triple Entente can simply be summed up with the old adage, "The friend of my enemy is my friend." Once more countries joined the Entente during World War One, it simply became known as the Alliance and the member countries as the Allies.

Lingering Resentments

While Britain's reasons for entering into the Triple Entente were practical and not personal, France's reasons were a healthy dose of both.

Yes, the French had practical reasons to join the alliance: Germany was their neighbor to the east and they wanted to check their aggression, as well as protect their colonial assets in Africa. But they also had a long-standing rivalry that bordered on resentment and even hatred. The French were still riled about losing the territory of Alsace-Lorraine to the Germans in the Franco-Prussian War (1870-1871) and many wanted to get that land back.

Still, others in France wanted to show that they were just as militarily capable as the more martial-minded Germans. French patriotism and nationalism was strong in the early twentieth century, to the point that some would say it was extreme.

The term chauvinism, which means extreme feelings for one's own group, is a French word and became more common in the English language after World War One.

The French had some old scores to settle with the Germans and if that meant entering into an alliance with their long-time enemies the British, then so be it.

Russia Needs Some Friends

So now we come back to Russia once more. Hopefully you are starting to see that Russia played an extremely important role in the events leading up to the war. Russians have traditionally been the least advanced and the poorest of all European powers, but there is no denying its geopolitical influence.

Russia's entry into the Triple Entente was also quite interesting. As discussed earlier, they were previously colonial rivals with the British and earlier fought against Napoleon and the French.

But for all the reasons Russia had to be against the French and British, it had just as many to be allied with Germany.

The Russian royal family was thoroughly infused with Germans and many of Russia's merchant and military class were ethnic Germans. The Russian military's high command often trained in Germany and learned the latest Prussian military tactics. Also, during the reign of Catherine the Great tens of thousands of ethnic Germans were invited to live in Russia as merchants, farmers, and bureaucrats.

Still, like the British, the Russians took a pragmatic approach to the situation, knowing that if the Germans attempted to acquire more land in Europe it would probably be at their expense.

And what about all those ethnic Germans living in Mother Russia, many Russians asked—could they even be trusted?

A Doomed Archduke

In 1914 the world was on edge. The combination of nationalism, colonialism, and the alliance structure meant that many people were expecting something big to happen. There was a feeling that war could break out at any time, anywhere, it was just a matter of how.

There were even some people trying to start a war.

Militant Serbian nationalists living in the Austro-Hungarian Empire began thinking that violence was the only way their people would ever be united with the independent nation-state of Serbia. They believed that if they did something big, then the world would take notice and possibly some of the bigger countries, namely their Slavic brothers in Russia, would come to their aid.

They set their sights on Franz Ferdinand (1863-1914), the Archduke of Austria-Hungary.

You may have heard of the doomed archduke Franz Ferdinand at some point in your life. Obviously, he had quite a memorable name, so much so that a rock band even named itself after him. But the real Franz Ferdinand was a somewhat complex and truly tragic figure in world history.

Franz was born into the German-speaking Hapsburg royal family that ruled Austria-Hungary and in 1914 he was the heir apparent to the imperial throne. He was born into a life of luxury and privilege, traveling the world, hunting big game, and being *given* a high rank in the Austria-Hungary military. He married his wife Sophie in 1900 and the two shared many adventures. His beliefs were a mixture of old world and new, which made him somewhat complex.

Franz was an ardent believer in monarchy, but he also didn't have a problem working with his empire's democratically elected leaders and showed no signs that he intended to transform the constitutional monarchy into an absolute monarchy.

When it came to the numerous different nationalities in his empire, such as the Serbs, the archduke's views were somewhat paternalistic. Franz believed that in helping the smaller and poorer groups by allocating resources to those regions, but he also thought that the German-speaking people should retain most of the control of the government and the others should defer to them.

With that said, Franz also favored creating a third crown for the empire, a Slavic crown, which would have given the Slavs of the empire more representation in the nobility and no doubt would've severely dampened militant nationalism by the Slavs.

Needless to say, not everyone in the Austro-Hungarian Empire agreed with the archduke's sometimes conflicting views on the direction of their country.

The Straw that Broke the Camel's Back

The events that took place in June 1914 in the Austro-Hungarian Empire were both ironic and tragic.

On June 28, 1914, the archduke and his wife were doing a tour of the city of Sarajevo (now in Bosnia), which was in the heart of Austria-Hungary's Serb and Bosnian territory. The plan was for the glamorous archduke and his beautiful wife to visit a military barracks and the city hall. Despite the influence of nationalism, the archduke and his wife were actually quite popular with the local population who viewed them as somewhat sympathetic.

But not everyone in Sarajevo liked them.

When it was announced that the archduke would visit

Sarajevo, a militant Slavic nationalist group known as the Black Hand began preparations to assassinate the royal couple. Led by a Serb named Gavrilo Princip, the plot involved six assassins, many more collaborators, and two attempts on the lives of the royal couple in one day.

The first attempt was a bombing, which managed to kill several people in the royal motorcade, but didn't harm the royal couple. The Archduke and his wife continued their tour of the city and were even on their way to the hospital to visit the survivors when nineteen-year-old Princip rushed their car with his gun blazing, killing both Franz and Sophie.

Within months most of the conspirators were caught—they were given sentences ranging from three years to death by hanging. Princip was given twenty years, but it may as well have been a death sentence. He was abused in prison, contracted various illnesses, and wasted away, dying in 1918 and only weighing eighty-eight pounds.

But the more important matter was how Austria-Hungary was going to react on a geopolitical level.

War is Declared

July 1914 became known as the "July Crisis" because it involved political and diplomatic posturing by countries from both alliances. Most of those involved wanted to avoid any undue bloodshed, but the government of Austria-Hungary looked at the matter a little differently — their blood had been shed, now it was time for retribution.

The Austrians already knew about the existence of the Black Hand and that Serbian politicians and military officers were among its members, but when they learned that some of the archduke's assassination conspirators were being harbored in Serbia their decision to attack the small country was all but decided.

The Austro-Hungarian government sent the Serbian government a list of ten demands that needed to be met to keep them from declaring war. Since the demands essentially amounted to Serbia ceding much of its sovereignty to the Austrians, they refused.

Austria-Hungary declared war on Serbia on July 28, 1914, thereby starting World War One.

The alliance system then went into effect when Russia declared war on Austria-Hungary and Germany countered by declaring war on Russia. France and Great Britain then declared war on Germany, setting the scene for the second largest, and what was at the time the greatest war in human history.

RANDOM FACTS

1. The Ottoman Empire officially entered into World War 1 on the side of the Central Powers when it attacked Russian ports on the Black Sea on October 29, 1914.

2. Italy's desire to acquire more land in central Europe at Austria-Hungary's expense was driven in large part by nationalism. Italian nationalists wanted to incorporate Italian speaking areas of the Austro-Hungarian Empire, especially Tyrol, into the Kingdom of Italy.

3. There was considerable hostility toward the British in their colony of South Africa by the Dutch-descended people known as the Afrikaners or Boers. The hostility came from the Anglo Boer Wars (1880-1881; 1899-1902), where the British conquered the Afrikaner nation-states of Transvaal and the Orange Free State, placing entire Afrikaner families in concentration camps in the process.

4. The territory of Alsace-Lorraine is west of the Rhine River, which France considered to be the boundary between it and Germany. The Germans, though, considered the region to be part of greater Germany because most of its inhabitants spoke a dialect of German.

5. France's government at the start of World War One was known as the "Third Republic." The First French Republic lasted from 1792 until Napoleon declared France an empire in 1804. The Second Republic lasted from 1848 until Napoleon III declared another empire and the Third Republic was then established in 1870 when the Second Empire fell during the Franco-Prussian War.

6. The Ottoman Empire's ruler for most of World War 1 was the Sultan Mehmed V (1844-1918).

7. Most of France's African colonies were in the northwest part of the continent, including Algeria and Morocco.

8. Russia's colonies once extended into North America, including Alaska and even a claim to parts of what are today the Pacific Northwest states. The United States bought Alaska from Russia in 1867. Some vestiges of Russian colonialism can still be seen in Alaska, such as the name of the town of Sitka.

9. Britain's vast empire was not always so easily controlled. Besides the well-known American Revolution and the Boer Wars mentioned earlier, the British had to deal with numerous revolts in India and other parts of Africa. They also conflicted with the Australian Aborigines and the

Maori people of New Zealand in the nineteenth century.

10. Austria-Hungary's geography sometimes created as many problems as its diversity. Located in central Europe, the Austro-Hungarian Empire was covered in mountain ranges that sometimes made transportation and communication difficult in the late nineteenth and early twentieth centuries.

11. By the late nineteenth century, the British colonies of Canada and Australia had developed cultural identities that were based on Europe, but due to the distance from the motherland, they were also unique. By the early twentieth century both were only nominally in the Empire, on a voluntary basis under "dominion" status. Together with South Africa and New Zealand, the four countries were often referred to as the "white dominions."

12. Russian expansion into the mineral-rich Caucasus region began in the late eighteenth century and continued steadily for about a century. The countries and kingdoms of Armenia, Georgia, and Azerbaijan became part of Russia during this period.

13. The Russian explorer Vitus Bering first landed in what would later become Alaska in 1741, thereby marking the beginning of Russia's brief imperial ambitions in North America.

14. Although the Monroe Doctrine explicitly stated that European powers couldn't get involved in the politics of independent American nations, it didn't say anything about the few colonies that still existed in North and South America. The British continued to hold on to colonial possessions in the Caribbean, as well as British Honduras in Central America (now Belize) and British Guiana in South America. The colony of British Honduras is the reason why Belize is the only English speaking country in Central America today.

15. Japan entered the war almost immediately on the side of the Triple Entente. It mainly fought the German navy in the Pacific, seizing German treaty ports.

16. Very few German citizens moved to the German colonies in Africa, with the exception of German South West Africa. Namibia still bears some marks from its past as a German colony, such as the name of the coastal city of Swakopmund.

17. Hungarians are often mistakenly thought to be Slavic, but their ancestry and language is known as Magyar, who were a non-Indo-European people that arrived in central Europe in the ninth century AD as warrior invaders.

18. Although many people in Europe, maybe most, thought that the world was moving toward a

general war, no one foresaw the assassination of the Austrian archduke as the ultimate catalyst. Because of that, some people today classify Franz Ferdinand's assassination as a "black swan" event.

19. During World War One, Bulgaria was a constitutional monarchy like most of the other belligerents on both sides. Despite its small size, Bulgaria boasted of a well-equipped army and a key central position to attack the Balkans or Russia.

20. After Germany was unified in 1871, it became known as the Second Reich, or empire. The First Reich was the Holy Roman Empire and the Third Reich was Hitler's Germany.

Test Yourself – Questions and Answers

1. Which country entered World War One first?

   a. Germany
   b. Austria-Hungary
   c. France

2. What did the Monroe Doctrine do?

   a. Prohibited European powers from engaging in colonialism in the Americas
   b. Invited Europeans to colonize Latin America
   c. Set Asia aside for future development

3. When was the Archduke of Austria-Hungary assassinated?

   a. June 28, 1914
   b. June 28, 1915
   c. June 28, 1918

4. In the mid-nineteenth century, the Ottoman Empire became known as?

   a. The Greatest Empire
   b. The Great Man of Europe
   c. The Sick Man of Europe

5. Along with France and Great Britain, the other original member of the Triple Entente was?

   a. Italy
   b. Russia
   c. The United States

Answers

1. b
2. a
3. a
4. c
5. b

CHAPTER TWO

THE EARLY WAR

When World War 1 finally broke out in the summer of 1918, Europe had entered uncharted territory. True, wars had engulfed the entire continent in the past, such as the Napoleonic Wars, but people knew that the Great War, as it was called at the time, would bring so much more destruction. The civilian population would be adversely affected and warfare would not be confined to Europe.

But that is not to say that none of the belligerents hadn't planned for the situation.

As we will see, some of the countries involved, such as Germany, developed highly detailed strategies, while others, such as Russia, seemed to rely on the rather unscientific strategy of throwing waves of soldiers at the enemy.

The Schlieffen Plan

If you know anything about European history then

you probably know that traditionally the Germans, and more specifically the Prussians, have earned reputations as great military thinkers. It is not that the Germans have necessarily been the most successful in warfare among their European cousins, but that they have philosophized about the art, or science, of war more than others.

Perhaps the greatest German war philosopher was Carl von Clausewitz (1780-1831), who wrote the book *On War*. Clausewitz examined war not only from a scientific standpoint, but also from a psychological perspective, exploring how intangibles can play a role in victory or defeat. He believed that wars were won through planning and that often the battle is decided even before the first shots are fired.

This was precisely the philosophy of the German high command before World War One.

The German generals and admirals began planning for a continental war long before the hostilities broke out in 1914, eventually coming up with what became known as the "Schlieffen Plan." The Schlieffen Plan was named for German Field Marshal Alfred von Schlieffen (1833-1913), who before the war even started envisioned that Germany would probably have to fight on two fronts. His plan called for the majority of the army gathering on the western front, flanking the majority of the French forces and their fortifications through Belgium. Once the French were defeated, the German army could then focus its energy on the numerically superior but technologically inferior Russian army to the east.

But things don't always go as planned.

Kinks in the Plan

You've probably heard or even said the term, "the best laid plans of mice and men often go astray." In the case of the German Schlieffen Plan this was certainly the case, which is ironic when you consider that one of the underlying themes of Carl von Clausewitz was to expect the unexpected.

In the first month of the war, it actually looked like the Schlieffen Plan was going to work as the German army raced across the fields of Flanders in Belgium, making it to the outskirts of Paris by early September. If the Germans could take Paris, then the war would be over. And to the older generation of Germans who were still alive and remembered the Franco-Prussian War, they thought it was going to be a repeat. The Germans were ready to drink plenty of beer in celebration and when that went dry they could drink all the champagne of the conquered French.

But there were a few important things that they didn't take into consideration.

Perhaps the primary point that the Schlieffen Plan missed was the scope of the conflict. Although it did consider that Germany would be fighting a two-front war, the reality is very different than theory. The plan incorrectly gauged that the Russians would be more of a nuisance than a legitimate foe, so when the Russian forces made deep penetrations all the way to the borders of Germany and Austria-Hungary in 1914 and 1916 the Central Powers were caught off guard.

The Germans also didn't think the French would give them as much resistance as they did, nor did they realize the impact that the British army would have on the western front.

After constructing elaborate defensive trenches and fortifications, the French and British made their stand at the Marne River.

The First Battle of the Marne – September 6-10, 1914

As the German forces cut across Belgium like it was hot butter, the French and British forces dug in north of the Marne River. They waited anxiously for the German juggernaut to arrive and when it finally did, the First Battle of the Marne began.

The bloody battle was like nothing witnessed before in Europe, or the world for that matter. Nearly 70,000 Germans were killed and more than 80,000 of the French and British died in the nearly week-long vicious trench fighting. Although the French and

British lost more men in the battle, they repulsed the German advance, which resulted in the Allies first decisive victory on the western front.

The front lines changed very little in the west after the First Battle of the Marne. Trench warfare and the use of chemicals became the norm, but we'll get to that later in our story.

A Family Affair

One of the more unique aspects of World War One was the fact that the royal families of Britain, Germany, and Russia were all related through marriage and blood. Queen Victoria of Britain (1819-1901), for whom her rule from 1837-1901 was dubbed "the Victorian Age," made sure to enmesh herself and her family in the affairs of Europe through a series of dynastic and power marriages. During the period of her rule, France, which was no longer a monarchy, was Britain's biggest competitor, so the queen decided to cozy up to Germany.

Victoria married a German prince named Albert, had a large family, and cemented British ties with Germany in process. Her eldest grandson was Wilhelm II (1859-1941, the Kaiser of Germany, who was therefore the first cousin of King George V of the United Kingdom (1856-1936).

The Tsar of Russia, Nicholas II (1868-1918), was the

first cousin to Wilhelm II and also had blood ties to the Danish, Greek, and British royal families. In fact, Nicholas II was actually more ethnic German than he was Russian.

The Austro-Hungarian nobility was deeply tied to the German nobility, which meant that by extension it was also connected to the British and Russian royals.

The only royal family involved in World War One that had no marriage or blood ties to the other families was the Ottoman royal family.

Although the royal families of Europe had connections with each other that were sometimes deep and strong, it wasn't enough to stop the war. The reality is that Europe no longer had absolute monarchs when the war began and therefore important decisions concerning warfare were dealt with primarily by the respective countries' democratically elected assemblies.

Why Did the Germans Wear Those Pointed Helmets?

World War One may not evoke the visual images that World War Two does, but if there is one image that probably comes to your mind it is those funny looking pointed helmets that the Germans wore. The image of those helmets, which were known as *Pickelhaube* or *Pickelhelm* helmets, has actually become very common in modern society. You may have seen some bikers wearing them in a cheesy 1970s exploitation film or maybe in the earlier novel and film *All Quiet on the Western Front* and if you are now reading this you are probably interested enough in World War One to ask: what were the origins of those helmets and what ever happened to them?

The Pickelhaube helmets originated in Prussia during the nineteenth century. Prussia was the largest and most martially orientated of all the German kingdoms of the time – they valued marching and looking good in their uniforms almost as much as their battlefield victories. The efforts to unify Germany also came from Prussia, so after Germany unified and entered into the Second Reich phase its military adopted a very Prussian character.

Thus the German spiked helmets of World War One.

The helmets were originally made of leather, but with the heavy use of artillery they were later made of steel. In 1915, the spike on the helmet was manufactured as detachable and later that year it was eliminated altogether. The ever pragmatic and thrifty Germans realized that the spike was a waste and served no real purpose.

By 1916, all German soldiers were wearing the steel *Stahlhelm* helmet, which was also used by the Germans in World War Two.

The Eastern Front

The Western Front is by far the most known of all the fronts of World War One. Although the majority of the battles and casualties took place on the Western Front, other theaters of operations were as important in determining the eventual outcome of the World War One.

The Eastern Front presented both problems and opportunities for the Central Powers. There were several opportunities for them to take land from Russia, from the Crimea region in the south all the way up to Finland in the north.

After all, the desire for more land was one of the primary factors for the start of the war so it would stand to reason that a major push would be made on the Eastern Front. But the Russians were not going to go so easy and although their infrastructure was inferior to Germany's and they were technologically behind Germany and Austria-Hungary, they did have the benefit of a large pool of soldiers.

And perhaps most importantly, Russia is a vast landmass. If the Central Powers thought they were going to roll over Russia quickly they only needed to look at Napoleon's failed invasion of Russia in 1812, or Sweden's similarly disastrous venture to conquer Mother Russia in 1707.

Following the Schlieffen Plan, the Germans

concentrated their forces in the west and let the Austrians attack Russia in the east, which didn't work so well initially. The Russians fought harder than expected and actually drove the Austrian and the German forces to the German border. But just when it looked as though the Russians had a chance to march into Berlin, their lack of infrastructure and technology proved to be their Achilles Heel.

The Russian forces got too far in front of their supply lines, which were unable to catch up with the front lines due to a lack of proper railroads in eastern Europe. A lack of telegraph lines also meant that the Russian high command was unable to effectively communicate with the troops on the ground.

All of these problems, combined with some superb strategic decisions by German field marshal and later chancellor of Germany, Paul von Hindenburg, led to a crushing Russian defeat at the Battle of Tannenberg (August 26-30, 1914). The Russian general who oversaw the debacle, Alexander Samsonov, killed himself in disgrace and from that point on the Russians fought a purely defensive war.

Russian soldiers, although often underequipped, often acquitted themselves well in a number of later battles, but you could say the war was over for them at Tannenberg.

The War in Africa

Outside of Europe, sub-Saharan Africa and the Middle East were the other two major theaters of operations during World War One. The Germans were heavily outnumbered by the Allied forces in Africa, which were primarily comprised of British and French forces along with their colonial auxiliaries. British and French forces quickly overran the German colonies of Togoland and Cameroon, occupying them completely by early 1916.

The situation was not so easy for the Allies in eastern and southern Africa, though.

In the Union of South Africa, many of the Afrikaners still remembered the Boer Wars and resented the British for their harsh treatment. They only reluctantly and with much reservation accepted colonial status in the British Empire with many looking for any chance to take back their freedom.

Many saw World War One as just that chance.

Manie Martiz was an Afrikaner/Boer nationalist, a veteran of the Second Boer War, and an officer in the Union of South Africa's army when World War One began. The South African command ordered him to move his units into German Southwest Africa, but he disobeyed the order and went over to the Germans. He then called on all Afrikaners/Boers to also come over to the Germans. He managed to get about 12,000 to follow him in what became known as the Martiz Rebellion.

The rebellion was ultimately unsuccessful, though, as most Boers remained loyal to the British Empire, taking Southwest Africa from the Germans in 1915.

Maritz was captured after the war and sentenced to three years in prison for treason, but only served three months when a sympathetic government took power in South Africa.

The colony of German East Africa fared much better, holding out for the entirety of the war even though it could only field 15,000 men against a combined Allied force of 100,000 men.

The War in the Middle East

Another theater of operations during World War One that you probably don't know much about took place in the Middle East. It involved two old allies—the Ottoman Empire and Britain—who were now involved in a fight to the death over the region. At the outbreak of the war, the Ottomans controlled most of the Arabian peninsula, Mesopotamia, and Palestine, while the British held Egypt. The British wanted to cut the Turks off from their oil fields and drive their forces the shortest way into Turkey, which meant following the coastline of Palestine.

But the Turks weren't going to go quietly.

As their German and Austrian allies were engaged in major offensives on the Western and Eastern fronts of Europe, the Ottomans launched their own major offensive in February 1915. The Ottoman offensive involved sending most of their forces through Palestine to invade Egypt, thereby vanquishing the British from the Middle East.

The Ottoman advance was stopped at the Suez Canal and then the British regrouped and slowly made their way north through Palestine, gaining Arab allies along the way by appealing to their emerging nationalist views.

As the British slowly worked their way north, the Ottomans also had to deal with a British invasion into Anatolia/Turkey from Greece.

The Gallipoli Campaign

As the Ottomans launched their campaign to take Egypt from the British, the British, French, and their colonial allies launched a campaign into the heart of Ottoman territory. After a sea bombardment that began in early 1915, the British, French, and many of their colonial allies attempted an amphibious invasion of Turkey on the Gallipoli Peninsula, which became known as the Gallipoli Campaign.

The Gallipoli Campaign was a disaster for the British.

After nearly a year of fighting, the Allied forces were

forced to retreat, handing the Ottomans their only true victory in World War One. The Allies limped back to Europe having suffered nearly 300,000 casualties. The campaign did become known for the heroic stand of the ANACs—the Australia and New Zealand Army Corps.

The British were able to take the region by the end of the war, but their initial loss gave the Central Powers a great boost of morale.

Lawrence of Arabia

You've probably heard about Lawrence of Arabia at some point, possibly having seen the 1962 film *Lawrence of Arabia*; but what do you really know about him and how he played a pivotal role in World War One?

Lawrence of Arabia was born Thomas Edward Lawrence in 1888 in Wales. For the remainder of his life he was known simply as "T.E." and from a young age he demonstrated incredible intelligence and curiosity. When he was in his twenties, Lawrence worked as an archaeologist on digs in Palestine and Egypt working with some of the most accomplished archaeologists of the period, including Flinders Petrie.

But ever the adrenaline and adventure junky, Lawrence eventually went to work for British intelligence using his archaeological work as a cover.

The Arabic speaking Englishman was able to gain the trust of Hussein, the Grand Sharif of Mecca, convincing him that a revolt against the Ottomans would be in his and his people's best interests. He then served as the military advisor to Emire Faisla, Hussein's son, and traveled with him on many adventures and missions throughout the Middle East.

Lawrence and his Arab allies used a combination of standard military maneuvers and guerilla attacks to harass and cripple Ottoman supply lines meant for the front lines against the British.

Eventually, Lawrence help lead his Arab allies in direct attacks against the Ottomans that were coordinated with the British Army's thrust into Palestine, with the capture of Aqaba on July 6, 1917 perhaps being his greatest achievement. He then coordinated more attacks, helping the British take Amman and Damascus in September 1918 by taking considerable pressure off the British front line.

After the war, Lawrence returned to England where he received acclaim for his deeds. Tragically, and perhaps somewhat ironically considering the dangerous life he lead during World War One, he died in a motorcycle accident in England in 1935 at the age of forty-six.

The Armenian Genocide

War is certainly a terrible thing. When you look at the reality of war and consider the lives and resources it costs, wars are far from being the glamorous events they are sometimes portrayed as in movies. In the modern era, wars have increasingly affected civilian populations, often resulting in massacres and even genocide.

World War One was no different than other modern wars in this respect.

Although you may think more of World War Two when you hear the words "genocide" and "civilian massacres," World War One was unfortunately when one of the first and largest genocides took place in the modern world — the Armenian Genocide.

Although the Armenian Genocide began in 1915 when the Ottoman government began systematically rounding up and murdering all ethnic Armenian men of fighting age, you could say that it began hundreds of years earlier.

The Armenians may live in the Middle East/central Asia, but they are closer to Europe and Russia culturally. Their language, like most European languages, is in the Indo-European family of languages and they are among the oldest of Christian communities in the world, unlike most of their neighbors who converted to Islam. During the First

Crusade (1095-1099), the Armenians controlled territory in what is today Syria and they proved to be solid allies to the European Crusaders.

In modern times, the Armenians fell under the control of the Ottoman Empire where during the best of time they were tolerated and in the worst of times they were persecuted.

After the Ottoman Empire entered World War One on the side of the Central Powers, its leaders decided then was the time to once and for all deal with the "Armenian problem." Deportations, massacres, forced marches, and forced mass starvations followed, resulting in the death of 1.5 million Armenians from 1915 to 1923.

In an era long before the Internet, news of the Armenian Genocide came out slowly. Ironically, it was a German medic named Armin Wegner serving in Ottoman-held territories who was responsible much of this information becoming public. Wegner wrote to American President Woodrow Wilson about the genocide and published a collection of his writings about the Armenian Genocide.

The modern Turkish government still hasn't admitted that the Armenian Genocide happened.

Why Trench Warfare?

You don't have to be Clausewitz or some other type of military genius to know that the idea of trench warfare seems counterintuitive, at least when it comes to modern warfare. It just doesn't seem very strategic to send a few hundred guys charging over an area the size of a football field only to get mowed down by machine guns once they got to the other side.

Well, there was actually a little more to trench warfare in World War One than that. True, modern depictions of trench warfare in World War One usually show it as a bloody battle of attrition where few men survived, but the reality was often different and the use of it during the war was quite legitimate and the culmination of ever-evolving military technologies.

As cannons and firearms were developed in the early modern period, castles, walls, and even armor became obsolete. Generals and military scientists began to think of new ways to stop, or at least slow down the charges of their enemies and to protect their troops from cannon fire. Trenches became a logical way to achieve those goals. A charging enemy force would obviously have to slow down when it encountered a trench system and cannons would have a mitigated effect, especially if the trenches were elaborate and built partially underground.

By the nineteenth century, trench warfare was common throughout Europe and was also employed in many battles during the American Civil War.

The strategy of trench warfare involved using a trench

system to protect your base, while a detachment of your army would then attempt to outflank your enemy's trench system. Trench fighting became the standard operation on the Western Front of World War One and in the early stages of the war they were quite simple, not unlike nineteenth-century trenches.

As the war went on, though, the trenches became much more developed. The Germans made a science out of trench building, often using concrete and adding ventilated bunkers to their larger systems. Most trench systems built by all belligerents had multiple trenches parallel with each other, with several smaller intersecting trenches used for communications. Cannons and heavy artillery would be placed in the back of the trench system.

Most trenches were a minimum of eight feet deep, which helped mitigate casualties from stray gunfire and snipers. One of the realities about how World War One trench warfare is often depicted is that the "no man's land" between opposing trench systems, which was what both sides were fighting over, was about the size of a football field.

Now that we have explored some of the basics of trench warfare, let's take a look at what it was like to live, fight, and die in the trenches.

Living, Fighting, and Dying in the Trenches

Fighting in the trenches on the Western Front was dirty, noisy, and above all dangerous. The mortality rate was an extremely high 10%, which is no wonder when you consider that landmines, snipers, and even traps were common. Because trench warfare was so physically and mentally draining, soldiers from all armies would usually spend about two weeks in the trenches before being relieved. Although there is a general perception that trench fighting involved mass frontal assaults, that is only partially true.

It is true that mass frontal assaults were common in the early stages of the war. Generally speaking, when a unit prepared for an assault they would all line up at the front of their trench system and then all rush at once when the commander blew his whistle.

The result was usually mass carnage and little change in the front line.

Finally, commanders on both sides realized that the mass frontal assaults were too costly and so began to develop nighttime assaults by smaller commando units. These commando attacks proved to be more effective, especially when used in coordination with other new technologies.

We will get to those new technologies in a bit, but for now let's take a look at one of the bloodiest trench battles in World War One.

The Battle of the Somme

The Battle of the Somme was fought from July 1 to November 18, 1916 on both sides of the upper Somme River in France. The battle was the first major mobilization of both sides, as about four and a half million combined soldiers fought on both sides. The Central Powers were represented solely by Germany, while Britain and France contributed nearly even numbers.

As big as the Battle of Somme was it was just as bloody. Trench fighting was the order of the day. Both sides built intricate trench systems that stretched for miles and were connected by smaller trenches and tunnels. The thinking was that that the side with the bigger trench system would win the battle but it only seemed to make the body count higher.

When the battle was finally over more than a million men were killed or wounded.

To make matters worse, the bloody battle was technically a draw as the front lines didn't change.

Hitler in the Trenches

One of the more infamous World War One veterans who fought in the trenches on the Western Front was Adolf Hitler. You probably know Hitler as the leader/dictator of Germany during World War Two, but did you know that he had a semi-distinguished military career during World War One?

Although Hitler was a citizen of Austria-Hungary, he was an ethnic German and a fervent nationalist so he volunteered for the German army. There is still some mystery surrounding how he was able to do that and not be drafted into the Austro-Hungarian army, but not long after the war began he was a member of the 16th Bavarian Regiment of the Imperial German Army.

Hitler saw major action in the First Battle of Ypres in October 1914 and watched as his company was reduced from 250 to forty-two men. He was promoted to Lance Corporal after the battle.

He then became a dispatch runner, spending most of his time behind the lines at the regimental headquarters. The post gave him the time to take many pictures with his unit and comrades. Some of the more interesting pictures show Hitler and some other soldiers from his unit with their regimental mascot, a pit-bull named Fuchsl.

Because the German army was always short of soldiers, Hitler was sent back into the trenches and was wounded by shrapnel at the Battle of the Somme. Towards the end of the war he was injured in a British gas attack and was later awarded medals for both injuries.

Hitler's war experience left him angry and with a deep resentment for the German leadership and those who wanted to end Germany's involvement in the war. He would later write about some of his wartime experiences in *Mein Kampf*.

RANDOM FACTS

1. The Maritz Rebellion in South Africa left over 100 people dead on both sides.

2. During World War One, the British had to deal with the Easter Uprising of 1916 in Ireland. Although the British were able to suppress the rebellion, it eventually led to Irish independence.

3. General Alexander Samsonov killed himself with one shot to the head from his revolver.

4. Communications systems could vary widely in the trench systems during the war. Some trench systems relied totally on human messengers, while some used telegraphs and more modern methods of communications.

5. The 1981 film *Gallipoli* starring Mel Gibson is about the ANZACs assault on the Gallipoli Peninsula in 1915 during the Gallipoli Campaign.

6. About 150,000 white South Africans fought for the British in World War One, most in the campaign against German Southwest Africa.

7. As the war dragged on and Hitler and his comrades were sent back to the front lines, Fuchsl and some of Hitler's sketches were lost.

8. It was rumored that Nicholas II of Russia may have had an affair with his first cousin, Princess Victoria of England.

9. T. E. Lawrence was initially reluctant to join the war effort, only doing so in 1915 after being convinced by leading British archaeologists and military officers.

10. More than 1 million Indians served overseas in World War One, fighting in Africa, the Middle East, and the Western Front. Members of the Sikh religious community, which is numerically small, were overrepresented per their share of the Indian population during the war.

11. ANZAC Day is celebrated every April 25 in Australia and New Zealand as their version of Veterans Day. It was initially done to commemorate the sacrifices of the Australian and New Zealand soldiers during the Gallipoli Campaign.

12. Aside from the intangible problems with the Schlieffen Plan—British involvement and the French and Russians fighting better than expected—the German high command didn't give the officers in the field enough units to complete the wide-sweeping flanking operation.

13. Traps used on the Western Front were usually low-tech but effective. Holes and pits covered

with debris and lined with spikes were common, just as they were in Vietnam.

14. Although many Romanians were citizens of the Austro-Hungarian Empire, there was an independent Kingdom of Romania when World War One started. Romania joined the Allies in 1916.

15. The British often conducted "trench raids," where they would steal enemy supplies and even letters to/from home by soldiers in order to gain intelligence.

16. Artillery served as more of a psychological rather than a physical weapon in trench warfare. Although artillery shells did kill, they often did little damage to the more intricate and better-built trench systems. Their noise and unpredictability, though, always kept the enemy off guard.

17. Cavalry was still used for combat in the early phases of World War One, but the combination of trenches and automatic machine guns made them obsolete. Horses were the primary way to move weapons, men, and goods during the war, as mechanized infantry was not introduced until World War Two.

18. Many Russians were initially quite supportive of the war effort because they wanted to erase the humiliating loss to Japan in 1905.

19. Many historians attribute Ottoman battlefield losses to Russia in the winter of 1915-16 to their preoccupation with carrying out the Armenian Genocide.

20. The Suez Canal was officially opened in 1869 and was not only of vital strategic interest to the British, but was the primary route through which most of its trade with India was conducted.

Test Yourself – Questions and Answers

1. What was Lawrence of Arabia's real name?

   a. T. E. Lawrence
   b. Lawrence Fox
   c. S. W. Lawrence

2. Which of these was *not* related to the major royal families of Europe during the war?

   a. Nicholas II of Russia
   b. Wilhelm II of Germany
   c. Woodrow Wilson of the United States

3. Which of these countries was *not* in the ANZACs?

   a. Australia
   b. New Zealand
   c. Canada

4. What type of attacks replaced full-frontal assaults of trenches?

   a. Digging/sappers
   b. Nighttime commando attacks
   c. Fire attacks

5. Where did the British stop the Ottoman advance in the Middle East?

   a. The Suez Canal
   b. The Panama Canal
   c. The Erie Canal

Answers

1. a
2. c
3. c
4. b
5. a

CHAPTER THREE

THE WAR DRAGS ON

As we discussed earlier, World War One was uncharted territory for the world and because of that no one really had any idea of what was going to happen next. Of course both sides hoped and many thought that the war would be over quickly, which was after all the purpose of the Schlieffen Plan.

But instead of ending quickly, new theaters of operations opened up in Africa and the Middle East and when Italy entered the war on the Allies side a third European front opened on the Italian-Austrian border.

By 1916, it was apparent to most people that the war was not going to end anytime soon.

So the generals and scientists from both sides began devising new ways to break the hopeless stalemate. The answers, or so they thought, was tanks, airplanes, zeppelins, submarines, and chemical weapons. But as you probably have already guessed, those things only break the stalemate when only one side has them, right?

The reality is that these new weapons only served to change the face of the war, leading to more deaths and bloodshed, often affecting innocent civilians.

Here Come the Tanks!

The combat tank has become such a ubiquitous part of modern armies that is now difficult to separate one from the other. Of course, tanks played a major role in World War Two, but they were only introduced to the battlefield in World War One in the middle of the war and made far less of an impact.

You might be surprised that the Germans, who were known for their tanks in World War Two, entered the tank race late in World War One and never produced anywhere near the number of French or British tanks.

Tanks were first used at the Battle of the Somme in 1916. Allied strategists believed that well-armored tanks could break through the trenches and protect advancing troops from automatic gunfire. It was also believed that tanks could easily go through barbed wire and over any traps in the no man's land. The theory was sound, but in practice it usually didn't work out so well.

The first tanks were developed by the British and French in 1915 and by the end of the war the British had produced 2,500 tanks and the French 4,000. In contrast, the Germans started later and had only put twenty tanks on the battlefield by the end of the war.

The final assessment of tank warfare during World War One is that the French tanks were largely ineffective—they were too slow, couldn't maneuver very well, and their armor was not as good as advertised. The British tanks were nominally better as they temporarily broke through the German Hindenburg Line and saw some success in the final push against Germany in 1918.

Still, the role tanks played in World War One was negligible. They never came through by ending trench warfare on the Western Front. It would be another twenty years before tanks would prove to be indispensable in land warfare.

Air Recon

Where tanks had little influence on the results of World War One, airplanes and zeppelins had a much bigger impact. Since the ancient Greeks, man had dreamed of one day flying alongside eagles, but it wouldn't be until the eighteenth century when man was finally able to do it in the form of a hot air balloon.

During the American Civil War and the Franco-Prussian War, balloons were used to spot artillery fire and for reconnaissance. Their effectiveness was open to debate since they couldn't fly very high and were obviously sitting ducks.

When the Wright brothers conducted the first motorized flight at Kittyhawk, North Carolina in 1903, everything changed. Within a few short years an airplane industry developed and by the time the war began both sides were developing ways in which to use aircraft. In the early stages of the war, airplanes and zeppelins (we'll discuss them more in-depth in a little bit) replaced cavalry as the standard method of conducting reconnaissance.

If the horses knew what was happening, though, they were probably happy. If you were a horse wouldn't you rather be hauling supplies back and forth instead of charging heavily defended trenches?

Due to radio limitations at the time, pilots would often make their observations, record them in notes, and then drop the notes behind their own lines. Zeppelin pilots would usually do the same.

In the early stages of the war, pilots from opposing armies usually didn't view each other as hostilely as soldiers on the ground did. It was common for opposing pilots to wave as they passed each other in the sky before making their observations.

As the war went on, though, both sides began to develop their aircrafts for offensive operations.

Death From Above

As the war continued and things began to look more desperate, both sides developed offensive air corps. Pilots started looking at each other not so much as equals simply working for another "company" as they had before, but as true combatants. Orders were given to pilots to take out enemy aircraft any way possible, which meant that they had to be creative.

The early World War One planes were not equipped with guns, so some of the first dog fights actually involved mid-air ramming. Pilots started carrying pistols and taking shots at each other in mid-air, but neither of those methods were obviously very effective, so engineers began developing guns that could be mounted on planes.

The first mounted guns could only be fired by the passenger seated in the second seat, but that simply wasn't good enough. Most planes were one-seaters, which meant the pilot had to have a gun that could shot forward without destroying the propeller.

The answer was the synchronized gun.

Both sides eventually developed synchronized guns, which were timed to fire without hitting the propeller, but the Germans first put them to use in the Fokker fighter planes in 1915. Of course the invention of the synchronized gun was more of an evolution than a finished product, as there were several accidents in the skies over Europe before the science was finally mastered.

Once the synchronized gun was mastered, a whole new culture of fighter pilots developed.

The Red Baron

You've no doubt tasted or at least heard of Red Baron pizza, but did you know it is named for actual World War One German fighter pilot? The Red Baron's real name was Manfred von Richthofen (1892-1918), who was from a well-connected, noble family. He is believed to be the first recognized combat "ace" (a pilot who claimed three or more air victories) and is actually credited with eighty air combat victories.

Beyond his combat prowess, Richthofen popularized the idea of pilots being glamorous. He was tall, handsome, suave, and sophisticated and always dressed well with a long scarf flowing in the wind.

After proving his ability in numerous battles, Richthofen was given command of a fighter wing, which became known by friend and foe alike as the "Flying Circus" due to the brightly colored planes. Richthofen usually flew a bright red plane with a large black iron cross, which combined with his noble background earned him the nickname the Red Baron.

As the Red Baron wrought havoc to the Allied forces, stopping him became a priority. While pursuing

Canadian pilot Arthur Brown, Richthofen was shot with one bullet that proved to be fatal. He was able to land his plane in an Australian held zone and when some Australian troops came to take him into custody he simply said "kaput" and died.

It is unknown who killed him; for years Arthur Brown was given credit for taking down the Red Baron, but recent evidence uncovered suggests that he may have been shot down by ground fire.

Not the Goodyear Blimp

Most of you reading this have probably seen the iconic Goodyear Blimp floating overhead at a major American sporting event. Today, the Goodyear Blimp and other blimps like it are little more than a novelty, but in the early twentieth century they were state of the vehicles and weapons of war. Although the Germans developed an air force during World War One that was led by pilots such as the Red Baron, they devoted most of their air resources, at least early in the war, to the development of a zeppelin —or as we call them today, blimps—fleet.

Zeppelins were the idea of German inventor Ferdinand von Zeppelin (1838-1917), who envisioned a large fleet of propeller-driven balloons, he called "airships," protecting Germany.

By the late nineteenth century zeppelins were in full

production and when World War One began both the German army and navy used them for reconnaissance in much the same way that airplanes were used, especially in the North and Baltic seas. Zeppelins could fly as fast as most aircraft at the time and were surprisingly maneuverable, but they used hydrogen to elevate, which of course is highly explosive in the right conditions. Despite the explosive nature of zeppelins, standard ammunition and artillery shells couldn't ignite them so the Allies later had to use explosive rounds specifically to take down zeppelins.

Of course, accidents could and did happen.

The most famous zeppelin accident was the peacetime 1937 Hindenburg disaster in New Jersey. In that incident, a passenger zeppelin named the Hindenburg caught fire after an explosion, killing thirty-six people. The cause of the explosion remains a mystery and has been the source of movies, books, and television shows, it even later inspired the name of the British rock group Led Zeppelin.

The idea to use zeppelins as offensive weapons came as the war grinded to a stalemate and coincided with the first uses of airplanes as weapons. The idea was to use zeppelins to drop standard artillery shells on enemy positions, but since they had to fly somewhat close to the ground and also due to their large size, they were quite susceptible to ground fire.

So the German high command decided to use them to terrorize civilian populations.

The first zeppelin raids on London took place in January 1915 and after 1916 zeppelin attacks were a regular occurrence. The same was true for Paris. Although the sight of large zeppelins approaching a city over the horizon and dropping bombs was certainly intimidating, they did little strategically speaking and the overall damage they inflicted was minimal.

Dreadnoughts and the British Navy

If there was one true "trump" card that the British held that could've broke the stalemate in the middle years of the war it was their navy. During the sixteenth century, when Henry VIII took some time away from killing his wives, he decided that since Britain was an island nation it needed to have the best navy in the world. From that point forward, Britain's navy ruled the waves and helped it become the premier imperial power in the modern world.

In the two decades before World War One, Germany was working overtime to build a navy that would at least come close to parity with Britain's. This is often cited by historians as a secondary factor for the causes of World War One because by the time war finally broke out Germany indeed had the second largest navy in the world. The British knew they had to make a move to stay ahead of the Germans on the high seas so they developed a new class of ship—the dreadnought.

The dreadnoughts were essentially the first true battleships of the modern era. They were fast, heavily armored, and equipped with plenty of cannons that allowed them to inflict damage on the sea or land.

The British naval strategy was to encircle Europe, at least on three sides, with their dreadnoughts. British dreadnoughts would patrol the North, Baltic, Mediterranean, and Black seas looking for German and Ottoman vessels.

The Germans were at an extreme disadvantage to begin with on the high seas: they had limited coastline and therefore fewer ports, they possessed few colonial ports, and their navy was smaller at the start of the war.

In order to find any hope of naval parity, the Germans looked *below* the waves.

U-Boat Warfare

The Germans knew that since they had little chance of building a fleet of destroyers to keep up with the British, they had to be a bit more creative so they decided to focus their naval resources on the fairly new technology of submarines. Submarines, known in German as *unterseebooten*, which is how they became known as "U-boats" in English, were propelled by diesel-powered engines and designed to strike quickly in the shipping lanes. The U-boats provided some unique advantages and also a few disadvantages to the Germans.

Perhaps the greatest advantage the U-boats had during World War One was that they were virtually undetectable by surface ships and even if a surface ship detected one there was little it could do before it was too late.

On the other hand, U-boats were much slower and less maneuverable than dreadnoughts. Also, due to technological limitations of the time, they had to sight their targets physically before submerging and firing.

Despite their limitations, German U-boats were responsible for sinking 5,000 ships, putting about 13 million tons of supplies to the bottom of the Atlantic. No British merchant ship was safe when U-boats were in the area and they were able to hunt the Atlantic at will until 1917 when the tide of the war finally changed.

U-151

Toward the end of the war, as things were getting desperate for the Germans, many in the German high command realized that something drastic needed to be done. Since the Americans were filling the void left by the Russians in the Allied forces, the Germans wanted to sock it to the Americans somehow, but doing so was easier said than done.

The United States was on the other side of the Atlantic, making it impossible to strike with the army.

But not with U-boats!.

On April 14, 1918, a large U-boat simply named U-151 left the port of Kiel, Germany for a three-month tour of the Atlantic that brought it to the United States' east coast. By the time it returned to Kiel in late July, it had sunk ten ships in American waters, laid mines in the Chesapeake Bay, and cut telegraph lines that connected New York and Nova Scotia. Although the damage U-151 did was minimal in the big picture, it was a reminder to many Americans on the east coast that they truly were in the middle of a world war.

A Chance for Peace?

In late 1916, after the Central Powers won some key victories, Germany made public offers of peace. The Germans and their allies were hoping to leverage their recent successes and the general slow grind of the war into an armistice that would benefit them. The Germans believed, wrongfully so, that the majority of the British and French population wanted to end the war as quickly as possible, no matter the price.

American President Woodrow Wilson offered to be a mediator in any possible peace negotiations, but before he could do so the Allies offered their own proposal to the Central Powers.

They wanted all lands before the war restored and also demanded reparations from the Central Powers and to essentially break up the Austro-Hungarian Empire. The Central Powers offered no response, though, so the war continued.

The Italian Front

When Italy joined the war on the Allies side in 1915, most of their forces were posted on their northern border fighting the Austro-Hungarian army. When you think of Italy, olive groves, sun, and nice beaches may come to mind. All of that may be accurate descriptions of some aspects of Italy, but not where the majority of the fighting took place in World War One.

The Italian Front took place high in the mountains, giving it the name of the "Alpine Front." The style of warfare was similar to that of the Western Front, particularly with the use of trenches, but the snow and cold temperatures added a whole other deadly dimension to the front. Many soldiers on both sides died of starvation, frostbite, and other weather-related ailments.

Although the Germans sent a few divisions to help their Austrian allies and the British and French sent some to aid the Italians, the vast majority of the fighting was between the Italians and Austro-Hungarians. Like on the Western Front, the front lines changed very little until the end of the war when the Italians were finally able to break through and decisively win.

Who Remained Neutral in Europe?

Although World War One had three European fronts and most nations of the world were involved, a small number of important European nations decided to stay out of the hostilities. The Scandinavian nations of Iceland, Norway, Sweden, and Denmark all decided to not get involved. It had been a long time since any of those countries were militarily relevant in the eighteenth century and even longer since the Viking Age; by the twentieth century the Scandinavians decided to focus their energies on commerce.

Spain, which was also far removed from its imperial heydays of the sixteenth through eighteenth centuries, also decided to refrain from the hostilities, along with always neutral Switzerland.

Perhaps the most interesting European neutral nation during World War One was the Netherlands. After Belgium broke away and became an independent nation during the early nineteenth century in the wake of the European nationalist surge, the Kingdom of the Netherlands consciously played a subdued role in the military affairs of Europe.

Once World War One began, the Netherlands declared its neutrality and the tiny nation of Belgium then became a battlefield. Since the Netherlands was so close to the action,its military was put on high alert but never used. Refugees as well as spies all made their way into the Netherlands during the war, but the Dutch were able to maintain their neutrality.

The Concept of Chemical Warfare

You have probably heard the term "war crime" at some point in your life and may be vaguely aware that there are actually "rules of war." The idea that wars have rules and that some armies follow them may seem counterintuitive. After all, the point of war is to kill more of the enemy, so why would it matter how it's done, right?

Well, as new technologies developed in the late nineteenth and early twentieth centuries that weren't initially meant for killing people, such as highly poisonous and caustic chemicals, some people in power thought that it might be a good idea to get agreements from leaders never to weaponize those chemicals. Most of the industrialized nations of the world came together in agreement at the Hague Declaration of 1899 and the Hague Convention of 1907 to "ban" the use of poisons in warfare.

Of course, bans such as those only work if everyone is on board, which was clearly not the case in World War One.

Strategists on both sides saw the use of chemical weapons as a way to break the stalemate of trench warfare. By the end of the war, nearly 51,000 tons of chemicals were used by both sides. The most common chemicals used were chlorine, phosgene, sulfur mustard (mustard gas), and tear gas.

Although chemical weapons proved to be very deadly and destructive, they were also difficult to control, which ultimately left their effectiveness of the battlefield open to debate.

The Second Battle of Ypres

The Second Battle of Ypres took place in Belgium from April 22 to May 15, 1915. It was part of the German offensive meant to flank the Allied positions in France, but like all other fighting on the Western Front it seemed doomed to be bogged down in bloody trench fighting.

But then a group of German chemists, led by Walther Nernst and Fritz Haber, proposed using chlorine gas to clear the trenches in the Ypres salient. The German high command agreed with the plan, so it was resolved to launch the mass chemical attack.

A prevailing wind allowed the attack to proceed, but

many of the French were prepared with protective masks.

The result of the Second Battle of Ypres was costly for both sides—the Germans suffered more than 30,000 casualties, while the French, British, and British colonials suffered more than 80,000 combined casualties. The Allied forces were able to stop the German advance, but the area around the town of Ypres was destroyed and became part of the front line.

The German chlorine attacks did quite a bit of damage, but did not carry the day for the German army.

Using Chemical Weapons

The process by which deadly chemicals were produced and used during World War One was actually fairly simple and straight forward. The chemicals would be produced in labs under orders from their governments and then handed over to the military, who would then "weaponize" the chemicals by putting them in mortar shells, canisters, or artillery shells. Small canisters could be used by individual soldiers but required the attacker to be close to the target and risked putting other attackers at risk of exposure.

Mortar shells allowed the attackers more distance but were less accurate than artillery shells, which by the middle of the war was the preferred method of both sides to deliver chemical weapons.

The obvious problem with using chemical weapons is that it can't be controlled. You can reasonably control where a bullet or an artillery round goes, but even when you have chemical weapons in the artillery round it doesn't necessarily mean that chemical will cooperate.

For the chemicals to be weaponized they needed to be converted to gas, which meant that they were subject to folly of the winds. Sure, the armies dispersing the chemical agents usually tried to do so only when they had favorable winds, but winds and weather can change quickly, which often resulted in an army suffering from their own chemical attack.

And the attacks were blistering.

The Horrors of Chemical Warfare

Mustard gas is probably the best known of the chemicals used in World War One because it was a blistering agent that left those affected with severe skin irritations and blistering, both internally and externally. Chlorine was easy to detect because of its distinct odor and green cloud, so it was often either mixed with or later replaced by the more deadly phosgene.

After chemical weapons became a regular part of the war, armies on both sides developed gas masks that had varying degrees of effectiveness and eventually "smell cases" that were used to not only detect the presence of chemical agents, but what specific chemicals had been used.

As both sides got more used to the use of chemical agents and better countermeasures were developed, the fear of them was diminished. It was then learned that sitting still in the midst of a chemical attack lessened the potential hazardous effects.

Chemical weapons claimed 1.3 million casualties during World War One, but only 100,000 fatalities, perhaps proving they were never really intended to kill. Chemical weapons were used primarily to sow fear and discord in the enemy, but also to inflict as much non-lethal damage as possible. Putting your enemies in hospital beds meant that your enemy had to devote more resources to their care and wouldn't be able to send those men back into the war anytime soon.

RANDOM FACTS

1. When U-151 ravaged the American east coast it was commanded by Heinrich von Nostitz und Jänckendorff.

2. The only German tank put into the field during World War One was the A7V, which needed a minimum crew of eighteen men.

3. After the war, Roy Brown, the Canadian who may have shot down the Red Baron, started a small airline company in Canada.

4. Although the British developed synchronized guns for their planes early in the war, the early models were unreliable so their pilots preferred to use wing mounted automatic guns until late 1917.

5. Since horses were still vital for moving supplies, various horse chemical masks were developed by both sides.

6. One strange development in the tank race was the invention of the "Tsar Tank" by Russian scientists Nikolai Lebedenko, Nikolai Zhukovsky, and Alexander Mikulin. It was so unusual because instead of using standard caterpillar tracks as all other tanks did, it had three wheels, two of them very large, which gave it the look of an armored tricycle.

7. Fritz Haber was a somewhat ironic personality associated with chemical warfare. He played a leading role in the development of Germany's chemical weapons program, but he was also a Noble Prize winner for inventing a process that synthesized ammonia from hydrogen and nitrogen gasses.

8. Combatants on both sides who entered the Netherlands were imprisoned. Early in the war many Germans entered the Netherlands by mistake, believing they were in Belgium.

9. The *strafexpedition* (punitive expedition) was a campaign launched by Austria-Hungary against Italy on the Italian Front in May 1916 that resulted in an Italian defensive victory.

10. The Battle of Jutland from May 31-June 1, 1916 in the North Sea between Britain and Germany was the largest naval battle in World War One. It involved about 250 ships and although was initially considered to be a German victory, the smaller German force lost many of its most important ships and was unable to go toe to toe with the British navy after that point.

11. Although many civilians on the Allied side considered the U-boats to be bloodthirsty marauders, which was bolstered by Allied propaganda, they were well-respected in Germany.

12. Ferdinand von Zeppelin traveled with the Union Army during the American Civil War as an observer.

13. The British Mark 1 tank was the first to see action in World War One.

14. Until early in 1917, American President Woodrow Wilson advocated for strict American neutrality in World War One, stating the United States "must be impartial in thought as well as in action, must put a curb upon our sentiments as well as upon every transaction that might be construed as a preference of one party to the struggle before another."

15. Dreadnoughts were actually just battleships that took their name from the first of its class, the HMS *Dreadnought*, which was launched in 1906. She survived the war, in part because she was not at the Battle of Jutland.

16. Although American propaganda depicted the Germans as barbaric in their use of chemical weapons, it was actually the French who first used tear gas against the Germans during the war.

17. The Red Baron began his military training at the age of eleven.

18. The Hague Convention of 1907, which banned the use of chemical weapons, was suggested by American President Theodore Roosevelt in 1904.

19. Mustard gas was so-called because when it was dispersed in aerosol form it usually had a yellowish color.

20. The first Allied bombing missions during World War One took place in September 1914 when British planes dropped twenty-pound bombs on zeppelin factories in Germany .

Test Yourself – Questions and Answers

1. What was the Red Baron's nationality?

   a. Austrian
   b. German
   c. Ottoman

2. Which country first used the synchronized guns in their airplanes?

   a. Germany
   b. Russia
   c. France

3. Where did the Battle of Jutland take place?

   a. The North Sea
   b. The Black Sea
   c. The Mediterranean Sea

4. London was first attacked with?

   a. Battleships
   b. Airplanes
   c. Zeppelins

5. Which was the most lethal chemical used as a weapon in World War One?

   a. Phosgene
   b. Tear Gas
   c. Mustard Gas

Answers

1. b
2. a
3. a
4. c
5. a

CHAPTER FOUR

INTERMISSION, THE BOLSHEVIK REVOLUTION

By now you probably know a lot more about World War One than you did before you started reading this book. You can see that there were some complex factors at work that led to it starting and as it dragged on many of the new technologies that people thought would end it sooner only helped kill more people.

And by 1917 things were not looking very good for the Allies.

As bad as things were on the Western Front, the situation was even worse on the Eastern Front. Russia was gripped by domestic turmoil and all but out of the war. Throughout the course of 1917, things moved so quickly in Russia that by the middle of 1918 they were no longer in the war and their more than 400-year-old royal family was wiped out in a minute. But as quickly as things happened in Russia, you could say that they were a long time coming.

A combination of Russia's poverty and tendency toward autocratic rule by its leaders led to extreme resentment toward the royal family by a large segment of the population. Other factors, such as Russia's multi-ethnic composition, relative isolation, and loss to Japan in the Russo-Japanese War also played a role in Russia becoming the world's first communist country and her withdrawal from World War One.

The Romanov Dynasty

In order to understand the events that led to Russia becoming communist and withdrawing from World War One, we have to go back a bit to the seventeenth century. In the late 1500s and early 1600s Russia was going through a period of anarchy and civil war. The previous dynasty had collapsed and various pretenders to the throne tried to take power. Three different men claimed to be Dimitry, the youngest son of Ivan the Terrible, and therefore the true heir to the throne.

None of them really were Dimitry and one was even supported by the Polish royal family.

After considerable conflict, a noble named Michael Romanov was elected by other nobles to be the new tsar, Michael I (ruled 1613-1645). The Romanovs brought stability back to Russia and even some amount of prosperity. Other notable Romanov tsars and tsarinas were Peter I (Peter the Great) (ruled 1682-1725) and Catherine II (Catherine the Great) (ruled 1762-1796).

As we discussed a little already, the Romanovs had a healthy dose of Germanic blood in their family tree. Catherine was herself a German princess and nearly every Romanov after her was of some German ancestry.

Despite the Romanovs' German background, saukerkraut and sausage were forbidden at the royal court. Well, not literally, but all the Romanovs were required to speak Russian and be members of the Russian Orthodox Church.

As the years went by, resentment against the Romanovs grew throughout Russia for a number of reasons. Nicholas I (ruled 1825-1855) was nearly overthrown in a military coup and Tsar Alexander II was assassinated in 1881.

It was clear that by the late nineteenth century Russia was once more an unstable country, so let's take a look at some of those reasons why.

Das Kapital

The political and economic theory of communism is an interesting concept in today's world. If you are forty-years-old or older, then you probably have memories of the Cold War and the threat of nuclear annihilation the Soviet Union posed. You also probably learned a few things about the communist system while you were in school. It was, after all, the antithesis to our own democratic-capitalist system, or at least that's what we were told.

If you are younger than forty, well, it's not really your fault if you don't know much about communism. The Soviet Union collapsed in 1991 and although China still claims to be communist in theory, it has certainly learned how to play the capitalist game quite well.

But it is important to understand the background of communism a little in order to understand how it affected Russia and World War One.

Like nationalism, communism was a new idea that arose in nineteenth-century Europe to challenge the old order. Unlike nationalism, though, it wanted to overthrow the entire free enterprise economic system, as well as all monarchies, and replace it with a "worker's paradise," often euphemistically referred to as the "dictatorship of the proletariat."

Communism as a political and economic theory can trace its origins to socialism, which is simply the idea that a government should provide certain services for its people. Socialism came out of the eighteenth century Enlightenment and the Industrial Age, but it was Karl Marx (1818-1883) who took socialism a step further into communism.

Marx was a German-Jew who believed that the workers should control all production and distribution, which is a bit funny considering that Marx was never a "worker" himself, always earning his living as a philosopher, writer, and academic. He believed that world history was a constant struggle between the haves and the have nots and that the only way to rectify this was to have a government of workers — the dictatorship of the proletariat — that controlled all finances. He articulated his views in books such as *The Communist Manifesto* and *Das Kapital*/Capital, which earned him many followers throughout Europe.

Eventually, Marx's views became known as "Marxism" and when applied in the political arena in the form of political parties it was known as "communism."

Communism always appealed more to educated intellectuals than the actual working class, but in countries like Russia, where severe economic problems were endemic and didn't seem to care much for the majority of the population, it could quickly win followers.

By the late 1800s, the Russian royals failed to grasp the problem that communism posed or how gained such a presence in Russia in the first place.

A Detached Monarchy

As the great political and economic changes swept through Europe in the nineteenth century, just like everything else, they came a little slower to Russia. The Russian royal family still ruled the country absolutely, unlike their cousins in western Europe who had far less power in constitutional monarchies.

And as the saying goes, "absolute power corrupts absolutely."

During the nineteenth century, the Romanovs tried using the political and social changes in Europe to their advantage. Instead of giving more representation to their subjects, though, they pursued a policy of ultra-nationalism. Russia is a vast country and has been home to several different ethnic groups for centuries, but by the late nineteenth century the tsars decided that it was time for them all to become Russian. The Romanovs banned schools from teaching in languages other than Russian and forced non-Russians, such as the Volga Germans, to serve in the military, all of which was part of the program of "Russification."

None of this helped Russia with its poverty and general backwardness compared to western Europe. The people in general continued to be poor and it was only in 1861 that serfdom was finally eliminated, about 300 years after most kingdoms in western Europe had done so.

The opportunity was ripe for communists, anarchists, and others to strike against the royal family. The assassination of Alexander II in 1881 was only the first strike.

Lenin, Trotsky, and the Boys

Steadily stirring the pot of revolutionary fervor and resentment of the Russian royal family was a core of revolutionary communists led by Vladimir Lenin (1870-1924), Leon Trotsky/Lev Bronstein (1879-1940), and others, including Joseph Stalin (1878-1953).

As has been already discussed, Russia's descent into revolution was a long process that was at least partially helped along by the tsars' myopic and somewhat dismissive attitudes toward their own people. In the late nineteenth and early twentieth centuries, those opposed to the tsars were many, but they were also disparate in their ethnicities and political views.

The ethnic Russians were of course the majority and were also the vast majority of the workers and peasants, but in the cities there were also a large number of Jews, Germans, Greeks, and various central Asian peoples, including Georgians.

The divergent political ideologies were almost as legion. The primary split among the radicals was the anarchists versus socialists, but among the socialists there were all various strains of communism. It came down to a cadre of well-educated activists to bring the groups together.

Vladimir Lenin was of mixed Russian ancestry and educated at Kazan University, which is where he became indoctrinated in socialist and communist ideology. He was an excellent public speaker and theoretician. He was complemented by Lev Bronstein, a young Jewish intellectual who was said to have been won over to Marxism by his first wife. After he became a revolutionary, he used the name Leon Trotsky to appear more Russian.

Since Lenin and Trotsky were basically nerds, they needed some muscle for protection on the streets, which is how they met Stalin. Joseph Stalin was born Ioseb Besarionis dze Jugashvili in the central Asian country of Georgia. Like Trotsky, Stalin gave himself the Russian surname Stalin, which means "steel."

So the trifecta of communism was born in the early twentieth century, but they still needed a few things to turn their way before they could come into power.

The Russo-Japanese War

As we discussed in chapter 1, Russia had been expanding its borders throughout the nineteenth century to keep up with the other European powers. Much of its expansion was into central Asia, but by the early twentieth century it was also expanding into Mongolia and northern China. You will recall that Russia sold Alaska to the United States, but it still wanted to keep an influence in the north Pacific region.

So did Japan.

Japan is perhaps one of the most interesting cases in modern world history. Essentially forced out of isolation and feudalism in the mid-nineteenth century by the United States, the Japanese quickly adopted Western technology and a semi-Western government known as the Meiji to fully modernize their country in less than 100 years.

The modernization of Japan was nothing short of a miracle.

The Japanese kept their unique culture, while adopting many Western attributes, including the imperialist drive. Many Europeans were impressed with Japan's quick transformation, but the Russians viewed the changes with suspicion, and rightfully so.

After plenty of bluster and some border incidents, war between Russia and Japan finally broke out on February 8, 1904. The Russian people initially rallied behind their troops and tsar, believing that they would make quick work of the "little yellow people."

The Russians were sadly mistaken.

The Japanese outperformed the Russians in nearly every battle and demonstrated superior nautical technology in the numerous sea battles. When the Russo-Japanese war finally ended on September 5, 1905, the Russians were utterly defeated. Russia was forced to hand over its possessions in China to the Japanese, as well as the strategic south Sakhalin Island.

The war confirmed Japan as a world power, giving them the right to sit at the geopolitical table with the Europeans and Americans. On the other hand, Russia's power and abilities became more openly questioned throughout the world. The British and French in particular questioned what type of ally they would make.

Back home in Russia, Lenin, Trotsky, and the boys saw Russia's loss in Asia as a potential gain for them and their movement.

The 1905 Revolution

As Russia's domestic problems continued to go unnoticed by the tsar and were exasperated by mounting battlefield losses in Asia in early 1905, thousands took to the streets in protest. And often leading those protests were Lenin and the boys.

The culmination of the unrest came on January 22, 1905, which later came to be known as "Bloody

Sunday." On that day, unarmed protesters, led by an Orthodox Christian priest, were marching to the Tsar's Winter Palace in St. Petersburg when they were fired on by the Imperial Guard. More than 200 protesters were killed in the violence, which threatened to get even worse.

Finally, in October, Tsar Nicholas II issued the "October Manifesto," which agreed to many of the protester's demands and paved the way for the Russian Constitution of 1906. It expanded the representative body of government, known as the Duma, by allowing universal suffrage. Although Nicholas II retained the throne, he was no longer an autocrat, which was more in line with the monarchies of western Europe.

By all accounts, Nicholas II didn't really care, but Lenin and the boys did.

Nicky and His Family

Perhaps the most tragic aspect of World War One was the murder of the Russian royal family. We'll get to that in a minute, but it is important to look for a minute at Nicholas II and his family. Nicholas II married a German princess named Alix in 1894. She was a devout Lutheran and not too keen to convert to Russian Orthodoxy, or to live in Russia, but after she married the young prince, and later tsar, she fell in love.

The couple had four daughters—Olga, Tatiana, Maria, and Anastasia—and a son, Alexei. The children were all attractive and by all accounts the family was very loving. Pictures and film show the family enjoying vacations and each other's company.

The images are important on so many levels. They help humanize the tragic Russian royal family, but also show their incredible ignorance at the same time. As Russia was about to go up in flames, Nicky and his family took trips on the Black Sea and played croquet at the royal palace.

Russia Enters the War

Since Russia was technologically and economically behind the rest of Europe in the late nineteenth and early twentieth centuries, it was required to spend a greater percentage of its resources on the military, which in turn led to economic problems, which in turn led to the rise of communism.

You get the point, right?

With that said, the Russian people are traditionally very patriotic and were ready to support their tsar and army. The Russian government was also pretty shrewd in its use of propaganda, years before the hostilities even began. The Turks, Germans, and Austrians were routinely depicted as bloodthirsty and greedy, while the Russians depicted themselves as innocent peasants.

But almost immediately after the first shots were fired, the many problems Russia had were manifested. Although the Russians had some able commanders and a multitude of young men willing to fight, the front line soldiers were woefully under-equipped. Many times there weren't even enough guns for every man in a unit. The best Russian officers were also underutilized with Russian offensives only being conducted according to the needs of the other Allies.

As mentioned earlier, logistics were also a problem.

Unlike the dense, trench fighting on the Western Front. The Eastern Front stretched for vast distances, requiring good communications and supply lines, which the Russians simply didn't have. When food was available, it often couldn't get to the front lines and if it did the perishable items were often spoiled.

After a series of setbacks in 1916, the Russian army was on the defensive and demoralized. The rank and file soldiers began listening a bit more to the communist propaganda that was making its way to the trenches.

Some were even deserting the army to join the cause.

The February Revolution

No doubt you've heard something about the "Russian Revolution" The event just celebrated its centennial and although not as well-known in the United States or the West in general, it was one of the most important events of the twentieth century and World War One.

But it was actually a series of events and specifically two revolutions.

The problems on the Eastern Front, combined with Russia's overall economic and social problems gave the radicals an opening. Various communist factions, such as the Bolsheviks, organized strikes in the largest cities' factories and mutinies became an everyday occurrence in February 1917.

After several battles between the tsar's police and protesters, Nicholas II abdicated his throne on March 2, 1917. The already existing Duma took over most of the powers of government, but was joined in power by the Petrograd Soviet. The Soviets were "workers' councils", comprised primarily of communist groups, such as the Mensheviks and the Bolsheviks. The new government was led by led by Alexander Kerensky, but almost immediately there were cracks in the shaky alliance.

The Bolsheviks and other more radical elements wanted to immediately end Russia's involvement in the war, officially dissolve the monarchy, and to redistribute the land.

To the Bolsheviks, it seemed as though things were business as usual.

The Bolshevik Revolution

Okay, so now we know the things were getting pretty desperate, unstable and complicated in Russia in 1917. All of this was music to the ears of the Germans, Austrians, and Ottomans, as they hoped that the unrest would force the Russians to formally withdraw from the war.

Lenin, Trotsky, and the boys also wanted to withdraw Russia from the war, but for different reasons. Although they were happy that the February Revolution removed the tsar from power, Kerensky was too *bourgeois* for their taste. In other words, the Bolsheviks thought Kerensky and the new government were too conservative, or liberal. Those modern political designations didn't really mean much back then. All you have to know at this point is that the Bolsheviks wanted to keep the revolution going.

They wanted complete power in order to build their workers' paradise.

Lenin returned to Russia from exile on October 10 and was soon joined by others, including Trotsky and Stalin. They immediately set to work to overthrow the government.

Now you may be wondering why the majority of the Russian people would join up with some homicidal communists like the Bolsheviks? Well, the Bolsheviks were far from a majority of the population. In fact, they were even a minority within Russia's far left of the political spectrum.

But they were the best organized and prepared organization in 1917.

The Bolsheviks were ardent revolutionaries and because of that everything they did was with the end goal of overthrowing the government in mind. They made connections in the military and took over the most important unions, such as the railway workers. Their heavy urban influence meant that they were able to control the streets of Moscow and Petrograd, which allowed them to take over the government.

On October 26, 1917, the Bolsheviks, led by Vladimir Lenin, took control of the Russian government. A few days later, on November 2, Moscow fell into their hands, which gave them control of the country's largest cities and industrial centers.

Brest-Litovsk

Almost as soon as it came to power, the Communist Russian government began negotiating a peace with the Central Powers. Now don't get the idea that the Bolsheviks like Germany, Austria-Hungary, or the Ottoman Empire. No, they saw them as "capitalist pigs" and probably even worse than the British and French.

But Lenin, who was then the dictator of the new government, was pragmatic if nothing else. He knew that it ran the risk of being toppled by a right-wing counter-revolution, or possibly within by other communists. So diplomats from Russia met with representatives from Central Powers in the town of Brest-Litovsk/Brest, in what is today the country of Belarus.

The agreement was quite simple. The Russians agreed to quit fighting and to renounce territorial claims in eastern Europe and the Caucasus region. The Central Powers agreed to likewise end their quest to further carve up Russia.

The treaty was signed on March 3, 1918, thereby officially ending Russia's involvement in World War One.

The Murder of the Romanovs

After the February Revolution, the leaders of the government faced the difficult proposition of what to do with the royal family. Some thought that they should be given some type of light punishment, while most thought they should be exiled.

The Bolsheviks thought they should all be executed, preferably in the most painful manner.

In the meantime, the provisional government decided to place Nicholas II and his family on house arrest.

For a time, the royal family lived in a palace and were treated quite well; they were allowed to keep many of their servants and had very little supervision. After the Bolsheviks came to power, things changed rapidly.

The family was transferred to the somewhat isolated city of Yekaterinburg, where their situation came to resemble prison more and more every day. Their servants were taken away and they were put on military rations. Then on July 17, 1918, the family was herded into the basement where they were held, lined up against the wall, and repeatedly shot and bayonetted.

Soldiers then took the bodies to a forest where they were mutilated and dismembered.

The Communists would make sure that the Romanov's burial site would never become a religious pilgrimage site.

Russia Forgotten?

Many people have the idea that once Russia went communist, it was all but forgotten in the West. This seems to be true because, unfortunately Russia's situation during or just after World War One is not very much in most schools.

In fact, Russia's involvement in World War One is certainly relegated to a lesser place of importance than that of the Western countries. But hopefully by now you know that just isn't true. Russia is Europe's sleeping giant—it's fine when it's sleeping, but once you start poking it you'll more than likely regret doing so.

So to answer the question simply, no Russia was not forgotten. But the question is a lot more complex. France, Britain, and the other Allies focused their attention on defeating Germany on the Western Front.

The Allies would let things continue in Russia until early 1918 when they thought they had to step in and do something. If Russia were allowed to descend into chaos, what would that do to the rest of Europe?

Civil War

When Lenin made peace with the Central Powers it bought him and the new Communist Party some time, but it didn't stop Russia's internal problems. Although the Communists held the major cities, the majority of the rest of the country remained out of their hands. Opposition movements began forming paramilitary groups, warlords starting taking land, and the Allies sent in troops in attempts to stabilize the situation.

Welcome to the Russian Civil War (1918-1921).

The Russian Civil War is known for its several different factions and the flags they flew. The Communists flew a red flag, which became symbolic for all communist movements throughout the world in the subsequent decades. The anarchists flew a black flag, militant peasants a green flag, and the tsarist/monarchists/nationalists, who were led by General Kornilov, flew a white flag. So the armies were often just referred to as reds, blacks, greens, and whites.

The Allies invaded from the periphery in order to stabilize the country and to presumably reinstall a western friendly monarchy, but never made much headway into the interior. Eventually, through some shrewd maneuvers and thanks to the divisions among their enemies, the Communists were able to wrest control of the country from all other factions as far east as Mongolia by 1921.

Lenin could then go forward with his plans to build the perfect workers' paradise.

A New Economic Policy

After claiming victory in the Russian Civil War, Vladimir Lenin introduced the New Economic Policy (NEP) to Russia. Two years of World War One, two revolutions, and three years of civil war had destroyed the Russian economy. Industrial production had dropped to one-seventh of pre-war levels and famine was widespread.

Millions of Russians were dead and many more were headed to their graves.

In the NEP, factory production was controlled almost entirely by the state, but agricultural was only taxed and not controlled. This was seen as a sort of olive branch by Lenin to the peasants, who fought the Communists during the Russian Civil War as the "Greens."

The NEP proved to be successful, as by the mid-1920s production levels were at pre-World War One levels. But Lenin would never enjoy the fruits of his program because he died in 1924.

Stalin would replace Lenin as dictator of Russia, but that is another story. . .

RANDOM FACTS

1. The term *tsar* or *czar* is a Russian language derivation of the word "Caesar." After the Western Roman Empire collapsed in AD 476, the greatness of Rome was considered to have been transferred to Constantinople, making it the "Second Rome." Constantinople was conquered by the Ottomans in 1453, but Ivan III of Russia (1462-1505) wanted to make Moscow the center of Orthodox Christian culture. He began referring to Moscow as the "Third Rome" and using the title of tsar.

2. Lenin's older brother, Alexander, became involved in a plot to assassinate Tsar Alexander III (ruled 1881-1894), but was arrested and executed on the gallows.

3. Before the Bolsheviks took Russia out of World War One, they were involved in the war and after the war was over they had to contend with their own civil war and foreign intervention. To deal with these situations the Bolsheviks enacted what was known as *War Communism*, where a fair amount of resources were dedicated to the war effort.

4. During its two-and-a-half years in the war, Russia

had four prime ministers, three foreign ministers, three defense ministers, and six interior ministers, which was either a consequence of or another reason for the country's instability, depending upon how you looked at the situation.

5. Nicholas II bore a striking resemblance to his cousin, King George V of Britain.

6. Karl Marx was exiled from Prussia in 1845 and then became a "stateless" person. He died in London, which is where his tomb is today.

7. After Alexander II was assassinated in 1881, official and unofficial pogroms forced thousands of Jews out of Russia and into Palestine. Jews were blamed as a group because many of the conspirators were Jews and communism in general was often viewed as "Jewish" by peasants and nobles alike due to its urban popularity and origins with Karl Marx.

8. After the Bolsheviks came to power, Kerensky was forced into exile. He first moved to France and then the United States and Australia before moving back to the U.S. where he died in 1970. The Russian Orthodox Churches in New York refused him a traditional Orthodox burial.

9. You've probably heard the Don McClean song "American Pie" and wondered what many of the lyrics meant. The song possibly makes a reference

to the Russian and Bolshevik revolutions: "And while Lenin read a book of Marx, the quartet practiced in the dark . . ." Since McClean has never thoroughly decrypted the song, though, we may never know for sure why Lenin was mentioned.

10. Among the territories that Lenin gave up in the Treaty of Brest-Litovsk were Finland, Latvia, Lithuania, Estonia, Belarus, and Ukraine. Lenin and the other leaders of the Communist Party didn't have a problem doing so, arguing that to keep control of those countries would be "imperialistic." Stalin, though, had no problem taking most of those countries back twenty years later.

11. As a young man, Trotsky attended a German language school in the cosmopolitan city of Odesa, which is located on the Black Sea.

12. When the conference was conducted, Brest-Litovsk was in German-held territory.

13. The grave of Nicholas II, his wife, and four of the children were discovered in 1979. A grave containing the other two children was discovered in 2007.

14. Several of the Romanovs and their servants had sewn their family jewels and other valuables to avoid being robbed by their guards. When they

were executed, the jewels served as shields from the initial onslaught.

15. Russian President Boris Yeltsin was one of the first Russians to publicly speak about the murder of the Romanov family after the collapse of the Soviet Union, calling it one of the most shameful events in Russian history.

16. Alexei's dog, Joy, was the only member of the Romanov family to live. He was discovered during the Russian Civil War by a British officer and brought back to England where he lived the rest of his life on a country manor.

17. The Russo-Japanese War began with a surprise torpedo-boat attack on the Russian fleet on Port Arthur, China. The naval base was one of the primary sources of conflict between Russia and Japan and was the site of a major siege during the war. The Russians surrendered the fort in December 1904 after a 148-day siege.

18. Not long after declaring war on the Central Powers, American forces briefly occupied the Russian city of Archangel on the White Sea in February 1918. The operation was conducted with Canadian forces under the auspices of the Triple Entente/Allied Forces, who wanted to stabilize Russia and possibly prevent it from becoming communist.

19. There was no Polish nation-state at the beginning of World War One. Most of what is today Poland, including Warsaw, was part of Russia, while the far western portion of the country was part of the German Empire.

20. Tsarevich (crown prince) Alexi Romanov was a hemophiliac and had to be constantly attended to by two sailors. Despite the extra attention, Alexi was constantly sick and in pain. Modern genetic testing shows that he inherited the ailment from his maternal grandmother, Queen Victoria of England.

Test Yourself – Questions and Answers

1. Which of these royal families was Tsar Nicholas II *not* related to?

   a. German
   b. Ottoman
   c. English

2. Brest-Litovsk is in which modern nation-state?

   a. Belarus
   b. Ukraine
   c. Finland

3. Where is Port Arthur located?

   a. Australia
   b. Korea
   c. China

4. Which of these men was the first dictator of Communist Russia?

   a. Joseph Stalin
   b. Vladimir Lenin
   c. Leon Trotsky

5. Which colored flag did the tsarists/monarchists/ nationalists fly during the Russian Civil War?

   a. White
   b. Green
   c. Red

Answers

1. b
2. a
3. c
4. b
5. b

CHAPTER FIVE

THE AMERICANS ENTER THE WAR

When the United States declared war on the Central Powers on April 6, 1917, the war was nearly over but far from being decided. In order to understand the importance of America's entry into World War One, let's go back a bit for a review.

Remember that in 1917 things were pretty much at a standstill on the Western Front. The tanks, chemical weapons, and airpower that leaders on both sides thought was going to make a difference didn't. And once the political situation in Russia began to deteriorate, it became clear to most that the Russians would be of little help to the Allies.

The outcome of the war was certainly in question in early 1917.

So when the United States entered the war on the Allies' side, they took over the role of Russia in many ways, providing support for Great Britain and France that finally allowed them to defeat the Germans in the west.

Many of you reading this are probably thinking: why did it take the United States so long to enter the war? The answer to that question is fairly complex and will be the subject of the next few sections. You have to understand that in some ways America in 1914 was very similar to America today—people were deeply divided on political and social issues. At the same time America was very different, especially when you consider that it had just emerged from its "wild west" phase of history.

A Rural America

If you were to travel back in time to the United States of 1914, you would no doubt be overwhelmed by how different it was compared to today. Depending upon where you ended up, you would probably be astounded by the open spaces and even if you were in a major city, it would be much smaller than those of today.

There were no endless miles of suburbs that transition into the exurbs. There were also no freeways spanning over metropolitan areas like spider webs as we have today. In fact, the Lincoln Highway, the first true intercontinental highway in America, was only finished in 1913 and large parts of it were little more than a dirt road. Although the United States was comprised of forty-eight states in 1914, making it a unified country from the Atlantic to the Pacific, it was still overwhelmingly rural.

The United States still is primarily rural in terms of landmass, but in 1914 most Americans lived in rural areas. Yes, there were a number of major cities, and those cities were growing rapidly due to a number of reasons, but most Americans still lived in small towns or in the country.

Mayberry was still a reality in 1914 America.

What this meant for the United States' involvement in World War One was that few Americans were concerned about events on another continent, thousands of miles away, across an ocean. Sure, some of these rural Americans had immigrant connections to Europe, which we'll discuss more in a bit, but many who did felt they left all those problems behind in the old country. The anti-German propaganda meant little to these rural Americans who were more interested in having new roads and telephone lines built in their counties.

And most of these rural Americans were civic minded and tended to vote for politicians who ran on anti-intervention platforms. If it were up to them, the United States would only fight in wars where Americans were directly threatened or could possibly benefit and the Great War didn't seem like one of those wars.

But rural Americans weren't the only Americans opposed to the United States involvement in World War One.

German-Americans

If you are an American reading this, there is a pretty good chance you have some German ancestry in your family tree. Germans make up the largest single ancestry group in the United States with more than forty-four million people and have been in this country since before independence. Germans fought on both sides of the American Revolution and after that war continued to come in great numbers until World War One. Between 1820 and the beginning of World War One, more than six million Germans immigrated to the United States, adding to an already sizable population.

The original German-Americans tended to settle in Pennsylvania, but by the mid-nineteenth century they were drawn more to the Great Lakes and Midwest states. Many became farmers in the Midwest, but others flocked to cities such as Chicago, St. Paul, St. Louis, Omaha, Minneapolis, and especially Milwaukee.

German immigrants were known to be very civic-minded, establishing clubs and organizations in their communities and becoming involved in politics from an early point, usually in the Democratic Party. German immigrants and German-Americans were loyal to their new country and many had no love for the German Kaiser, but few wanted to go to war against their brothers and cousins back in the Old World.

Many German-Americans also argued, "we came to America to get away from those wars."

Irish-Americans

Not far behind Germans, about thirty-three million Americans are of at least partial Irish ancestry. Most of the Irish began coming to American in the middle of the nineteenth century in the midst of famines and British oppression. The Irish brought with them a unique way of looking at the world's problems, some good whiskey, and a deep hatred of the English.

The Irish primarily migrated to major cities in the northeast and Midwest, but were somewhat more evenly dispersed than the Germans. Like the Germans, they tended to be loyal Americans and Democrats and often peacefully shared neighborhoods with German immigrants.

By the early twentieth century, many Irish had assimilated into the American mainstream, but large pockets of fiercely proud Irish neighborhoods that maintained close ties to the Old World remained in Boston, New York, Philadelphia, Chicago, and other cities.

And many of those ties were to the Irish independence movement.

In 1914, very few Irish or Irish-Americans wanted to go to war to help Britain. Like their German-American neighbors, many believed that the United States should stay out of European wars.

The Socialists

Leftist politics have historically played a much bigger role in Europe than in the United States. With that said, by the late nineteenth century numerous left-wing political groups, some pretty radical, began popping up in America. President William McKinley was assassinated by an anarchist in 1901, which caused the government to begin clamping down on some of those groups. Despite the actions of some radicals, socialism as a political philosophy became more popular in the early twentieth century.

The Socialist Party of America (SPA) formed in 1901 and almost immediately it attracted thousands of followers across the country because it addressed many new problems that been previously unthought of, which were the result of industrialization and a society that was becoming much more urban.

Although clearly on the left and using red as its color, the SWP stayed away from Marxist talk and never referred to itself as a communist, professing to be purely American.

Besides labor issues, the SPA was vehemently against any and all wars. It argued that wars only benefit the rich and that therefore the United States should stay out of the Great War.

SPA leaders such as Eugene Debs (who we'll get to in a little bit) made speeches deriding the British and French as being as bad as the Germans.

The Socialists may not have had the numbers to take over the government at the ballot box, but they did have enough influence to sway public opinion about the war.

Americans Who Favored War

Although many Americans opposed getting involved in World War One, there was an equally significant number who favored intervention. Most of those who favored intervention were generational Americans, with many being wealthy WASPs (White-Anglo-Saxon-Protestants) on the east coast. The WASPs had cultural and economic reasons for supporting the war. Many WASPs maintained contacts with family and friends in the British Isles and also did extensive business in that part of the world.

Besides, war could be good for business.

In 1914, there was no military industrial complex as there is today—no Lockheed Martin, Boeing, or Northrup—and there was no real standing army to speak of, but many of the east coast elites stood to make a nice profit selling steel and munitions to the British. The United States did not officially sell munitions to the Allies early in the war, but private American companies did extensive business with the British. The United States Cartridge Company and Baldwin Locomotive Works both had lucrative contracts with the British and Russians. For them the war was good business and would only get better if the U.S. were to declare war on the Central Powers.

Other than the east coast WASP elites, millions of other Americans believed that the British and French were fighting a moral fight on behalf of democracy against despotism. This idea was repeated in American propaganda posters, where the Germans were depicted as bloodthirsty "Huns."

Support for American involvement in the Great War was heaviest in the southern states, which had a far lower percentage of Irish and German immigrants.

The Evil Hun

As the war raged on, anti-Central Powers propaganda, especially anti-German propaganda, became much more common in the United States. A lot of the British propaganda made its way across the Atlantic, which often featured the Germans being referred to as "Huns."

But why were the Germans of World War One compared to a people who lived more than 1,000 years earlier and with whom they had no direct connection?

Well, it appears that there were several that combined to make the Germans the hated Huns of World War One.

You probably know that the Huns were led by a guy named Attila, which is kind of a tough name to begin with, and you probably also know that they were the terror of Europe for some time. Although the Huns were originally from Asia, they rode into Europe and began ravaging the Roman Empire in the early fourth century AD. Many of the Huns left and some were assimilated into the local populations, which is where the modern country of Hungary gets its name. The Huns left such a mark on central Europe that they, and especially Attila, became the subject of many ancient German legends.

The second reason probably has to do with the ferocity of the Huns. There is no doubt that the Huns were ferocious warriors, as they were known for killing entire populations. The comparison between the Huns of old the Germans in World War One began to be made after the Germans invaded Belgium in the first two months of the war. Many Belgians resisted with guerilla attacks, which resulted in harsh reprisals by the Germans against the civilian population in what became known as the "Rape of Belgium."

Finally, Kaiser Wilhelm II invoked the name of the Huns in a positive connotation when he gave a farewell speech to the German expeditionary force leaving to fight in the Boxer Rebellion on July 27, 1900. An English translation of the speech reads:

"When you meet the enemy, he will be defeated! No quarter will be given! No prisoners will be taken! Those who fall into your hands are forfeit to you! Just as a thousand years ago, the Huns under their King Etzel made a name for themselves which shows them as mighty in tradition and myth, so shall you establish the name of Germans in China for 1000 years, in such a way that a Chinese will never again dare to look askance at a German."

But in order for propaganda to be effective there has to be a certain level of truth behind it, right? Just calling the Germans Huns would've meant little to the average American. Even reading about atrocities committed against the people of Belgium wouldn't have mattered much to most Americans. There needed to be direct offenses committed against Americans or America.

Fortunately for the Allies, the Germans made more than one misstep that pushed the United States into the war.

The Sinking of the Lusitania

You no doubt know about the sinking of the *Titanic* because it was one of the greatest disasters to ever happen to a passenger ship in history. The tragedy was so terrible that countless documentaries and books were produced about it detailing how it happened, and of course there was that movie with Leonardo DiCaprio and Kate Winslet.

But just about three years later another maritime tragedy struck in the north Atlantic Ocean.

Let's go back to the U-boats for a minute. Remember how the British were trying to blockade the Germans with their dreadnoughts? Well, the Germans tried to do the same thing around the British Isles with their U-boats. Although the Germans had a policy of not attacking passenger liners, on the foggy night of May 7, 1915 they thought that the *RMS Lusitania* passenger liner, which was on its way from New York to Liverpool, was carrying munitions.

A single torpedo hit the ship, which in turn caused another explosion. It turns out that the ship probably was transporting some munitions; but it didn't really matter much once the details were made public. Out of nearly 2,000 passengers, 1,198 died, 128 of them

Americans. The scale and size of the disaster was nearly the same as the *Titanic*, with the obvious exception being that the *Lusitania's* demise was caused by human hands.

The Germans tried to justify their actions by pointing out that there were in fact munitions on the ship, but the damage had been done. It was a true public relations disaster for the Germans.

It was another straw in the camel's back that pushed American sentiment closer to war.

The Zimmerman Telegram

The final straw that broke the camel's back was actually a comedy of errors that involved an espionage plot that reads more like a spoof than a James Bond novel. It was perhaps one of the biggest mistakes the Germans made during the war and it didn't even happen on the battlefield.

To be fair to the Germans, though, in early 1917 it was beginning to look more and more like the United States would declare war on them. Americans were still angry about the *Lusitania* and the propaganda was starting to have an effect, pushing public opinion toward war. The German leadership apparently felt that there was nothing they could do to keep the Americans out of the war, so they opted for what they believed was the next best scenario—induce a country to attack the United States.

The Germans thought they had to look no further than Mexico. After all, the Americans had taken plenty of Mexican territory less than 100 years earlier and after Mexican rebel leader Pancho Villa had attacked New Mexico in 1916 the United States flexed its imperial muscles again by conducting an expeditionary mission onto Mexican soil.

So with all of this in mind, German foreign secretary Arthur Zimmerman sent a cable to the Mexican government enticing them to join the Central Powers. It stated that if the U.S. entered the war, Germany would help Mexico recover lands lost in the Mexican-American War of 1846-1848. Of course, the telegram never said how Germany would help them do that; there was little they could've done as most of their resource were stuck in Europe.

The Mexicans had too many problems of their own and decided that neutrality was the best course.

The British intercepted the telegram and handed it over to the Americans, all but ensuring that the United States would enter the war on the side of the Allies.

The Homefront after War Was Declared

Once the United States officially declared war on the German Empire on April 2, 1917. Because President Wilson and leaders in Congress believed that Germany was the primary threat, war was only declared later that year on Austria-Hungary. Once war was declared, most Americans fell in line with the war effort, although some didn't, which we'll get to shortly.

Pro-American and anti-German propaganda was produced in even greater volumes after the declaration of war and the government also enacted the Food and Fuel Control Act on August 10, 1917. The Act was carried out by a newly created Food Administration, headed by future president Herbert Hoover. The Food Administration had the power to set prices, license distributors, control exports and imports, and disseminate food related propaganda. The food-related propaganda included publishing a weekly calendar that detailed what foods Americans should or shouldn't eat on each day of the week: "meatless Tuesdays," "sweetless Saturdays," "porkless" Tuesdays and Saturdays, and "wheatless" Mondays and Wednesdays.

The government also promoted loyalty oaths and some would say spying on one's neighbors. German-Americans began suffering discrimination in some parts of the country and some were even subjected to violence. Because of this, many Germans and German-Americans Anglicized their names during World War One. For instance, Schmidt became Smith, Becker became Backer, Metzger and Fleischman became Butcher and so on.

Most German-Americans tried to keep their heads down and avoid conflict. Thousands loyally served in the army and the majority of the overall population did what they could on the homefront.

But there were some very vocal Americans who protested the war even after the United States joined the Allies.

The Espionage Act and the Sedition Act

The Socialist Party of America and their allies continued to vocally oppose the war, even after the United States joined the Allies. Although President Wilson was considered a "progressive", he was not happy with war protests.

Today, protesting war has become such a regular part of American culture that when the president even authorizes limited strikes on a country there are sure to be some protests. We commonly think of war protests as beginning during the Vietnam era, but the reality is that other wars were protested by Americans before Vietnam. Many in the northern states were opposed to fighting in the Civil War so much that draft riots broke out in New York City. So when protests against World War One took place, they were not necessarily new, but their organization was.

The government began to feel that the organizations behind the war protests were a threat, so Congress passed the Espionage Act of 1917, which was signed into law by President Wilson. The Espionage Act made it easier for the government to spy on dissenters, but that law was further beefed up when Congress passed and Wilson signed the Sedition Act of 1918. The Sedition Act basically made it criminal to protest the war.

The Sedition Act's most notable victim was Socialist Party of America leader and presidential candidate, Eugene V. Debs. Debs called for young men to resist the newly institute draft, which authorities used to charge him with sedition. He was convicted and sentenced to ten years in prison, but was released in 1921 when his sentence was commuted by President Warren Harding. The new president wanted to leave the scars of the war in the past.

The Selective Service Act

America's entry into World War One coincided with the period in American history known as the "Progressive Era." You may have heard that term used from time to time more recently in American politics, but the original Progressive Era took place in the early twentieth century, until about the time of World War One.

Progressive politicians, who were both Republicans and Democrats, believed that the United States had grown to such a point that the laws of the country, or lack thereof, needed to be updated and some added.

Most of the new laws and government organizations were meant to help the American people, such as the Food Administration discussed earlier, but not all did so as seen by the Sedition Act.

The United States military was another institution that the Progressives felt was archaic and in need of reform. In fact, there really wasn't much of a military to speak of. The United States only had a skeleton force of a standing army in 1917, so the government had to think of a quick remedy.

They instituted a draft.

The United States government had instituted military drafts previously, but the new draft in 1917 was a vision of the Progressives. Congress passed and President Wilson signed the Selective Service Act of 1917 into law on May 18, 1917. It authorized the federal government to draft an army, requiring all male citizens between the ages of twenty-one and thirty to register for a potential draft.

So now you know the origins of the Selective Service Act, let's see what impact it had on the war.

Here Come the Doughboys!

You may have heard the term "doughboy" somewhere in regards to World War One, but probably really haven't considered its origins or what it means. You may know that it referred to American soldiers in

World War One, which is true, but you probably didn't know that it was intertwined with popular culture of the era.

The term doughboy was first used to refer to American infantrymen in the Mexican-American War (1846-1848), with one explanation being that the soldiers were covered in dust and dirt that looked like dough from marching through the desert. By the time the United States mobilized for World War One, the term was used regularly and became a part of pop culture.

The Selective Service Act allowed the government to muster four million young men into service. As the young men were leaving stateside to uncertain fates in France, several odes were written about their sacrifice, the most famous being George M. Cohan's song, "Over There." The Lyrics follow:

First Verse:

> Johnny, get your gun, get your gun, get your gun.
> Take it on the run, on the run, on the run.
> Hear them calling you and me,
> Every Son of Liberty.
> Hurry right away, no delay, go today.
> Make your Daddy glad to have had such a lad.
> Tell your sweetheart not to pine,
> To be proud her boy's in line.

Second Verse

Johnny, get your gun, get your gun, get your gun.
Johnny, show the "Hun" you're a son-of-a-gun.
Hoist the flag and let her fly
Yankee Doodle do or die.
Pack your little kit, show your grit, do your bit.
Yankee to the ranks from the towns and the tanks.
Make your Mother proud of you
And the old red white and blue

Chorus

Over there, over there,
Send the word, send the word over there
That the Yanks are coming, the Yanks are coming
The drums rum-tumming everywhere.
So prepare, say a prayer,
Send the word, send the word to beware –
We'll be over, we're coming over,
And we won't come back till it's over, over there.

Fighting the Germans and the Spanish Flu

When the first American doughboys began arriving in late 1917, most were in for a severe culture shock. Most had never been out of their hometowns, never mind being in a different country. Remember, the United States was still an overwhelmingly rural country in 1917 and very few people outside of the elites took long trips for leisure. So needless to say, some of these American country boys had a bit of fun when they landed in France and first checked out libertine Paris.

And many of the Parisian women liked the American boys too.

But the fun of checking out new, exotic locales was quickly replaced with the uncertainty, adrenaline rushes, and accompanying fear of fighting in the trenches for the members of the American Expeditionary Forces (AEF), as the American Army was called during World War One.

Almost one million Americans saw action in Europe, which included a naval battle group, with around 100,000 losing their lives.

But did you know that only about half of those lives were lost on the battlefield? The other half fell victim to the Spanish Flu epidemic of 1918 while they were in Europe.

By some estimates, the Spanish Flu epidemic of 1918 killed up to 100 million people or about five percent of the world's population. People of all backgrounds and geographic locales were susceptible to the deadly disease, which caused havoc on the front lines during World War One.

Still, as men from both sides were dying from the flu, the war continued to rage. The Americans were supposed to help put the final nail in the Germans' coffin, but the stubborn Germans didn't seem to know the word surrender.

General "Black Jack" Pershing

John Joseph "Black Jack" Pershing (1860-1948) was the commander of the AEF during World War One. It only takes one look at a picture of the guy and a brief examination of his military record to see that he was a character, a man's man, and a true American original. He fought in the Indian Wars as a young man and charged up San Juan Hill in Cuba in 1898 with Teddy Roosevelt.

Of course, one of the most interesting things about General Pershing was his nickname: so how did he get it? Unfortunately, it looks like we'll never really know for sure, but there are two theories that seem fairly plausible. The first, and what many consider to be the most likely, is that he got the name when he commanded the black "Buffalo Soldiers" during the Indian Wars and the Spanish-American War. Another theory is that he acquired the name when he was an instructor at Army Academy at West Point. He was supposedly so rough on the cadets that they called him "nigger Jack" behind his back, which later became "black Jack."

Whatever the origin of the nickname, it stuck and by the time he led the AEF in Europe it was what he was known by.

Pershing's job in World War One was certainly not very easy. He had to essentially build an army from scratch and once he got it ready to take the field he had to deal with plenty of arrogance and some contempt from other Allied commanders. The British and French wanted all of the AEF to serve under them, but Black Jack strongly resisted. As a sort of compromise, he allowed the few black combat units to serve under the French, but the rest of the American units would fight under the stars and stripes.

By the time the Americans took the field, it was just in time because the Germans were attempting one last offensive.

The Germans' last gasp was their Spring Offensive, which took place from March to July 1918. The Germans threw everything they had left at the Allies and were able to take a considerable amount of real estate, but it proved to be a pyrrhic victory. Their numbers were severely depleted and their morale was diminished. On the other hand, the Americans fought well and proved themselves to their European allies. The heavy fighting also made veterans of the Americans who served in the campaign.

Black Jack was now ready to lead his troops to victory.

The Hundred Days Offensive

After the German Spring Offensive failed to win them the war, the Allied high command decided that now was the time to strike back at the Germans to end the war. The Ottomans and Austrians were all but defeated and if the Germans were toppled the other Central Powers would have no other choice but to accept surrender. With the Americans now in the field with hundreds of thousands of men, the Allies decided to throw everything they had at the Germans.

And the doughboys would play a major part in the final Allied offensive.

On August 8, 1918 the Allies attacked the complete length of the front lines, beginning the Hundred Days Offensive, which would last until November 8. The AEF played support roles throughout the front, but in the Argonne and St. Mihiel salient in the southern part of the front they played a major role. Between September 12 and September 16, AEF forces advanced out of St. Mihiel, pushing the Germans back into Germany and taking 16,000 prisoners. They also advanced to Sedan and in the middle of the front marched with the British to retake the Somme.

Although *direct* American involvement in World War One was brief, it was decisive as American manpower gave the Allies the numbers to finally defeat the Germans.

RANDOM FACTS

1. In 1900, Philadelphia, New York, and Chicago were the only American cities with more than one million inhabitants.

2. As an example of how the "Frontier Period" of American history had just ended when World War One began, William Frederick "Buffalo Bill" Cody had just ended his famous "Wild West" shows in 1895 and died on January 10, 1917, months before the United States entered the war. Also, Butch Cassidy and the Sundance Kid, thought to be one of the last of the frontier outlaw gangs, had pulled their final job in the United States in 1901 and were reportedly killed in South America in 1908.

3. Eugene Debs died in 1926 at the age of seventy from cardiovascular problems that many attribute to the time he spent in prison.

4. The *Lusitania* was a British flagged ship on its 202 voyage. It was bound for Liverpool from New York when it was sunk off the coast of Ireland.

5. The Food and Fuel Control Act was supposed to expire after the war, but it was made permanent and the Food Administration was expanded into the Food and Drug Administration.

6. George Cohan was born to Irish immigrant parents in Providence, Rhode Island in 1878. He began his music and entertainment career at the age of eight, performing on stage with his vaudeville parents.

7. When World War One began, there were more Irish and Irish-Americans living in New York City than in Dublin, Ireland's capital and largest city.

8. The Germans suffered 688,341 casualties to the Allies 863,374, but by that point it was no longer a numbers game. The addition of American troops meant that the Allies could continue the fight much longer than the Germans, who needed a quick and decisive victory.

9. Pershing was the only person to be promoted to the rank of General of the Armies during his lifetime. George Washington is the only other American general to attain that rank, which he was awarded posthumously in 1976 during the Bicentennial.

10. You've probably heard the saying that "things change quickly in politics," or something along that line. During World War One in the United States this was especially true. Woodrow Wilson was re-elected in 1916 partially on an anti-war platform, but within months of his second

inauguration he was leading the country into war.

11. In the United States, real wages rose by 50% from 1914 to 1918, proving once again that wars stimulate economies and can be profitable.

12. There was some opposition by southern politicians to include black males in the draft, but the War Department (the forerunner to the Defense Department) decided to go ahead and draft blacks. Although blacks were drafted, they served in racially segregated units. Blacks were excluded from the Marines and very few were drafted into the Navy, and only as laborers. Most black soldiers were also laborers, but the 92 and 93 Infantry Divisions were all-black combat units.

13. In 1910 the United States was the number one producer of crude petroleum and had the most railway mileage of any country in the world.

14. Some believed that the pickelhaube helmets worn by the German infantry in the first two years of the war resembled those worn by the Huns, Mongols, and other Asiatic steppe peoples, which was another reason why the Germans were called Huns.

15. The Spanish Flu pandemic was actually two pandemics that lasted until late 1920. It was the same H1N1 virus, often referred to as "swine flu," that hit the world in 2009-2010.

16. The Americans suffered 127,000 casualties (killed *and* wounded) during the Hundred Days Offensive.

17. Since the Sedition Act of 1918 was made law not long before the war ended, there were not many prosecutions under it and Debs was the highest profile offender. Congress repealed the act on December 13, 1920.

18. General Pershing led the American military expedition to capture Pancho Villa from March 14, 1916 to February 7, 1917. Although Pershing didn't capture Villa, he helped raise his national profile, leading to him becoming the commander of the AEF.

19. The Selective Service Act of 1917 was repealed when the war ended. The current selective service system in the United States is the result of the Selective Service Act of 1948.

20. Remember we talked about all the Allied powers invading Russia during the Russian Civil War? The Americans were also part of that operation. General Pershing sent the 27th and 339th Infantry regiments to Russia.

Test Yourself – Questions and Answers

1. Which was not a possible origin of General Pershing's nickname?

   a. He commanded Buffalo Soldiers
   b. He was a tough instructor
   c. He was an excellent blackjack player

2. What the name of Germany's final offensive?

   a. The Klink Offensive
   b. The Spring Offensive
   c. The Winter Offensive

3. Who was Eugene Debs?

   a. The American vice president during World War One
   b. Presidential candidate and leader of the Socialist Party of America
   c. The commander of the American Expeditionary Force

4. What country was the Zimmerman telegram sent to?

   a. Canada
   b. Argentina
   c. Mexico

5. What city was the Lusitania returning from when it was attacked?

    a. Boston

    b. New York

    c. Los Angeles

Answers

1. c
2. b
3. b
4. c
5. b

CHAPTER SIX

THE PEACE AND UNRESOLVED ISSUES FROM THE WAR

We've come a long way in our study of World War One. You now know that there were many issues that led to the war and many things that happened during its four years that earned it the moniker of the "Great War." But you really can't discuss World War One without discussing its "peace' and unresolved issues. After all, the Great War was supposed to be the war to end all wars, but just over twenty years later World War Two happened.

It didn't happen in a vacuum.

We'll see in the next chapter that many of the ideas put forth by the Allies after the war had the opposite effect of diminishing the prospect of future wars. The peace imposed on Germany was especially harsh and led to widespread resentment and economic collapse, which opened the door for political violence. The end of World War One also led to the formation of a new political world order, exemplified by the League of Nations.

The end of World War One had a different effect on the United States. As a result of American involvement, the United States would from that point forward play a much bigger role in international affairs, whether isolationists wanted to or not.

To the Victors Go the Spoils

Although the last shots of World War One fired were on November 11, 1918, the war was not officially over. The November 11 peace was officially an *armistice*, which set forth some broad terms for the unofficial peace: Allied occupation of the Rhineland, removal of all German troops beyond the Rhine, and the release of prisoners. The armistice began at 11 am Paris time and later had to be extended three more times.

Meanwhile, the leaders of Allied nations began meeting to discuss the terms they would impose on Germany for a permanent peace treaty.

There were essentially two conflicting philosophies in the Allied camp pertaining to the type of peace they would pursue. British Prime Minister David Lloyd George and American President Woodrow Wilson urged restraint. They argued that Germany should be reintegrated into the European economic system as quickly and as painlessly as possible. They further added that holding grudges would be counterproductive and lead to more rivalries and possibly war.

You're probably thinking, "yeah those guys were right!" But hindsight is 20/20 and it was somewhat of an easy position for the British and Americans to take considering that no battles were fought on their soil.

Sure, the British and Americans, especially the British, lost plenty of men in battle and Britain was attacked by zeppelins, but it just wasn't the same amount of damage as France sustained.

French Prime Minister Georges Clemenceau wanted to hurt Germany. He wanted to cripple Germany militarily, economically, and politically and he didn't really care what effects it would have on the rest of Europe or the world for that matter. In fairness to Clemenceau, though, it was what the majority of the French people wanted as well. Two wars with Germany in less than forty years was enough, so they thought that by severely crippling their rival it would never happen again.

Wilson and George got Clemenceau to ease up a bit on some of his demands, but in the end the peace that was created truly crippled Germany.

The Treaty of Versailles

The Treaty of Versailles was the treaty that officially ended World War One, and make no mistake about it, it was *imposed* on the Germans. At the Paris Peace Conference where the treaty was formalized and finalized on May 7, 1919, German Foreign Minister, Count Brockdorff-Rantzau was presented with the document and told to sign. He wasn't happy with the peace, nor were many in Germany, but it was essentially up to the military command. They told the government to accept, which it did on June 28, 1919 in the famous palace of Versailles.

The terms of the peace were even worse than most Germans imagined.

Germany lost 13% of its territory overall, including some areas in the west going to Belgium, Alsace-Lorraine was returned to France, the city of Danzig and the "Polish corridor" were given to a newly reconstituted Poland. Remember, there was no Poland nation-state at the beginning of World War One as all Polish speaking people were either part of the German or Russian empires.

The Rhine Valley was also occupied by French troops. It was bad enough to lose a lot of their land, but having French troops occupy one of the most prosperous parts of their country was too much for many Germans. They didn't like the idea of any foreign power occupying part of their country, but many thought, "why couldn't it have been the Brits or the Americans? Anyone but the French?"

The Germans were also forced to pay 132 billion marks in reparations, fixed in 1921 to prevent payment with inflationary marks. The Germans had sixteen billion marks in overseas assets seized and German rivers were forced to be open to international traffic.

Finally, the German army, the pride of the nation, was all but disarmed. The army was capped 100,000 men who were on long-service contracts and all training schools were closed.

It was certainly far different than what you would see today after a way. In the modern world when wars end, the victor often rebuilds the vanquished, dedicating immense resources to the project. Not so after World War One.

So France got its wish to impose a harsh peace on Germany, but did it help?

Problems with Versailles

After the harsh peace of Versailles was imposed, it was like the rest of the world just forgot about Germany. The rest of the world, especially the United States, went into an economic boom in the 1920s and just didn't seem to care anymore about what happened in World War One.

But the Germans had no choice but to deal with their situation.

The harsh economic penalties of the Versailles led to a round of hyperinflation—where the cost of commodities increase by 1,000% or more—from 1921 to 1923. The new government based in the city of Weimar seemed powerless to stop it and weak overall.

Germans began turning more and more to fare left-wing and right-wing political parties for answers and political street violence became a regular occurrence—hundreds died in political violence in Germany during the 1920s.

Eventually, you know what happened. Well, if you don't be sure to check out my World War Two trivia book to learn.

The Fate of Austria-Hungary

We've talked a lot about Germany and how it was dealt with after the war, but you are probably wondering what happened to Austria-Hungary and the Ottoman Empire, right? Well, their situations differed and in many ways were worse than what happened to Germany, at least for those in power.

Toward the end of the war, President Wilson unveiled his "Fourteen Points," which was his plan for post-war Europe. Unfortunately for Austria-Hungary, especially the nobility, they weren't a part of those plans. In fact, Wilson called for the full independence of the various nationalities within the Austro-Hungarian Empire.

The Allies never really had to impose a harsh peace on Austria-Hungary. The country began to disintegrate in the final months into its constituent parts, with new countries being formed as a result. The monarchy was dissolved, Austria, Hungary, Czechoslovakia, and Yugoslavia became new countries, and the Polish regions were joined to the newly formed country of Poland.

The internal dissolution of the Austro-Hungarian Empire was driven by a somewhat strange alliance of nationalists and leftists and was supported by outside forces, namely the Allied nations.

There was still one more empire the Allies had to dissolve if the war was going to be truly over, though.

The Fate of the Ottoman Empire

The Ottomans ended their involvement in World War One on October 30, 1918 when they agreed to the Armistice of Mudros. Although the Ottoman Empire was already on life support when the war began and was not likely to be a threat in the future, the Allies wanted to make sure of that.

The Allies immediately occupied the Ottoman capital of Istanbul and set to work to partition the Ottoman

Empire. Dividing the Ottoman Empire proved to be a bit more difficult, though, than what took place in Austria-Hungary. In the case of Austria-Hungary, the various nationalities that later formed nation-states had well-established independence movements and plenty of leaders who were educated in some of the best universities in Europe.

This was not the case with the Ottoman Empire.

The majority of the non-Turkish nationalities in the Ottoman Empire were poor and illiterate, so the European powers thought it would be better if they stepped in to run things for a while.

Imperialism and the rich oil fields of the Middle East may have also played a role.

We'll get to how the European powers ended up with the Ottoman colonies in a minute, but for the time being let's look at what happened to the Ottoman Empire next. Since it lost nearly all of its non-Turkish territories, the Ottoman Empire couldn't properly be called an empire anymore, but it did still have its sultan. Well, they had him until he abdicated his throne on November 17, 1922. A few months later, on July 23, 1923, the remnants of the Ottoman government then signed the Treaty of Lausanne with the Allied powers, which officially ended the Ottoman Empire and recognized the Republic of Turkey.

The partitioning of the empire's constituent parts would for the most part be handled by the League of Nations.

The League of Nations

Another one of the direct results of World War One that came out of the Versailles Treaty was the formation of the League of Nations. You probably know something about the United Nations, but most people know a lot less about the League of Nations because it was ultimately a failure.

The League of Nations officially formed in 1920 and dissolved after World War Two, but it quit being a serious organization by the 1930s when stronger nations realized that it couldn't or wouldn't enforce any of its decisions. One of the big reasons cited for the failure of the League of Nations was the United States' refusal to join. By the 1920s the American economy was doing very well and Americans had slipped back into their isolationist attitude — Americans just didn't have time for some silly international organization.

One of the most significant things the League of Nations did was to divide up the German and Ottoman empires into what were known as *mandates*. Since France and Britain were really the only two remaining colonial powers in the world and since both countries already had colonies in the Middle

East and Africa, most of the mandates were given to them.

Most of the mandates went smoothly with most of the countries attaining full independence during or after World War Two.

But in some places, things only seemed to get more complicated.

The Balfour Declaration

By now you can probably see that there is no clear line dividing the end of World War One and the beginning of World War Two. Sure, we know exactly when the last shots were fired in World War One and when the first shots were fired in World War Two, but the events that ended the first and led to the second are clearly blurred. But the events that happened as a direct result of World War One not only led to World War Two, but also events much later.

The Balfour Declaration is one such World War One event whose repercussions are still being felt.

On November 2, 1917, when the fate of World War One was still far from being decided and British troops were furiously fighting the Ottomans in the Middle East, former British Prime Minister wrote and signed what became known as the "Balfour Declaration." The Balfour Declaration essentially stated that the Jews of Palestine in the Ottoman Empire should be given their own state once the war was over. It was a non-binding letter, but it had widespread support among Europe's Jews, especially Zionists, and in the major political parties of Britain.

Once World War One was over, the Balfour Declaration set off a massive wave of European Jewish migration to Palestine, which forever changed the demographics of the region, eventually leading to conflicts between the Jews and British and then between the Jews and Arabs.

Today, many of the issues created by the Balfour Declaration still exist and show no signs of going away anytime soon.

Veterans Day

When the doughboys came home from their service in World War One they were rightly regarded as heroes. November 11 became known as "Armistice Day" when President Wilson proclaimed it as such. He wrote:

ADDRESS TO FELLOW-COUNTRYMEN

The White House, November 11, 1919.

A year ago today our enemies laid down their arms in accordance with an armistice which rendered them impotent to renew hostilities, and gave to the world an assured opportunity to reconstruct its shattered order and to work out in peace a new and juster set of international relations. The soldiers and people of the European Allies had fought and endured for more than four years to uphold the barrier of civilization against the aggressions of armed force. We ourselves had been in the conflict something more than a year and a half.

With splendid forgetfulness of mere personal concerns, we remodeled our industries, concentrated our financial resources, increased our agricultural output, and assembled a great army, so that at the last our power was a decisive factor in the victory. We were able to bring the vast resources, material and moral, of a great and free people to the assistance of our associates in Europe who had suffered and sacrificed without limit in the cause for which we fought.

Out of this victory there arose new possibilities of political freedom and economic concert. The war showed us the strength of great nations acting together for high purposes, and the victory of arms foretells the enduring conquests which can be made in peace when nations act justly and in furtherance of the common interests of men.

To us in America the reflections of Armistice Day will be filled with solemn pride in the heroism of those who died in the country's service, and with gratitude for the victory, both because of the thing from which it has freed us and because of the opportunity it has given America to show her sympathy with peace and justice in the councils of nations.

WOODROW WILSON

The holiday was expanded after World War Two to include commemorating all American war veterans and therefore renamed "Veterans Day."

Luckily, World War One veterans didn't have to deal with some of the negative attitude veterans did in later wars, especially Vietnam, but their experiences were often downplayed by most Americans. People expected the veterans to quickly reintegrate themselves back into society, but many found it difficult to do.

Shell Shock

You've probably heard the term "shell shock" at some point, but have you considered what it actually means or its origins? The term originated in World War One and was used to describe physical and psychological problems soldiers acquired on the front lines. It was first recognized and termed by the British, but as you're reading this there is a good chance you're thinking, "this sounds like post-traumatic stress disorder (PTSD)."

You are right.

Shell shock is what military officials called PTSD decades before PTSD was identified as a legitimate ailment. The militaries of World War One had an extremely difficult time dealing with cases of shell shock and some British soldiers were even jailed and executed for cowardice.

But of course the shell shock didn't end when the soldiers returned home from the war. Many soldiers had difficult times finding work, dealing with their families, and generally reintegrating back into society, which sometimes led to alcoholism and suicide.

World War One shell shock/PTSD is even depicted in the 1987 American television film *The Man Who Broke 1,000 Chains* starring Val Kilmer. Unfortunately, as bad as shell shock was for many World War One vets, it was largely forgotten when the United States went into an incredible economic boom during the 1920s. Although booze was banned, there was plenty of money around for everyone to party with and people just wanted to forget about awful things like the war.

The Bonus Army

The booming economy and good times of the 1920s gave way to the Great Depression of the 1930s and the people who were perhaps hit hardest were the World War One vets. As many vets struggled to find their place in society during the 1920s, the onset of the Depression made things even worse. Many felt slighted by their own neighbors, friends, and family members and to add insult to injury it seemed as their own government had forgotten their sacrifices.

The government was refusing to pay World War One vets wartime bonuses.

A grassroots and decidedly right-wing movement began in the 1920s for the vets to get their bonuses. The American Legion was the largest organization to advocate on behalf of the veterans' wartime bonuses, but neither political party seemed to listen so the veterans decided to take things into their own hands.

They followed the long American tradition of marching on Washington, which is how the "Bonus Army" was born.

About 17,000 World War One vets, along with their friends, family members, and various others sympathetic to their cause, for a total of 43,000 people, gathered in Washington, D.C. on July 28, 1932. They set up a tent city and planned to stay there until they were paid what they believed was owed them.

President Hoover responded by sending in the army to tear down the tent city, which resulted in two dead and many injured. The situation was a political disaster for Hoover, who would be a one-term president, and garnered much sympathy for World War One vets.

President Roosevelt proved to be much more sympathetic to the Bonus Army; they were finally given their bonuses in 1936.

All Quiet on the Western Front

There's a good chance you're familiar with the German novel, *Im Westen nichts Neues* (In the West Nothing New), by German World War One vet Erich Maria Remarque. You may have read the book under its English title *All Quiet on the Western Front*, or have seen either the 1930 film or the 1979 television movie starring Richard Thomas (he played the character John Boy in the 1970s television show *The Waltons*) in the lead role.

The book and subsequent films follow the perspective of a German soldier as he is subjected to all the horrors that came with fighting on the Western Front, particularly in the trenches. Far from glorifying war as most war-themed books had done previously, *All Quiet* showed the pain that war causes and the often futile nature of it all.

All Quite on the Western Front was also one of the first books to explore the psychological effects of war, delving into the concept of shell shock/PTSD.

The book and films went on to international acclaim and helped create a dialogue about war, pacifism, and coexistence in an increasingly volatile world.

Ernst Jünger

The gritty realism of *All Quiet* was reflected in the memoirs of German World War One infantryman, Ernst Jünger. Titled *Storm of Steel* (*In Stahlgewittern*), the reader follows Jünger through his dangerous time on the Western Front, as he is wounded time after time, but keeps returning to the front to do his duty.

Storm of Steel differs from *All Quiet* in that there is an absence of judgment. Jünger is not interested in preaching to the reader, or telling his views about war, but he only wants you to experience a part of what he felt during that time.

In fact, in some ways Jünger almost takes a positive view of war. He seems to see it as a challenge to be overcome and referred to it at one point as a "great adventure." It should be pointed out that most of the more positive references to war were in the early chapters where he and his fellow soldiers idealistically go off to fight and die for the fatherland.

But there is no doubt that *Storm of Steel* was devoid of political commentary, which is one of the reasons why it escaped censorship during the Nazi regime while *All Quiet on the Western Front* did not.

Frank Buckles

When you look around today, there aren't many veterans from World War Two still alive. The youngest Americans to have served in World War Two would be around ninety-years-old today, so it goes without saying that all of the World War One vets are now deceased.

But how long has that been and when did the last doughboy die?

Thanks to state of the art record keeping, we know that the last American World War One vet to die was Frank Buckles on February 27, 2011 at the age of 110! Frank enlisted in the army at the age of sixteen and served as an ambulance driver on the Western Front. Buckles had quite an interesting life after the war as well. He worked for a private contractor in the Philippines and was captured by the Japanese when they took those islands over in 1942 during World War Two. He became a leader of the POWs in the camp and was finally released in 1945 when the Americans liberated the island.

Buckles moved back stateside, married, and had his only child at the age of fifty-four.

He remained healthy and active well past his 100th year of life, meeting President George W. Bush and leading a Memorial Day parade with actor and activist Gary Sinise in 2007.

Truly, Frank Buckles embodied the spirit and determination of all doughboys.

Post Script: The Balkans War

Among the several and interconnected effects that World War One had on the world, one that is often overlooked is the Balkans War/Yugoslav Wars that took place from 1991 to 2001. Think back to what we learned about the Austro-Hungarian Empire, namely how it was comprised and eventually how it dissolved. One of the countries that formed was Yugoslavia, which in many ways was just a smaller and more Slavic Austro-Hungarian Empire.

As the name denotes, Yugoslavia was a nation-state of Slavic peoples, envisioned in the era of nationalism and formed from the ashes of World War One. Many thought it would work because all of the constituent peoples were Slavic, but the differences, and sometimes hatreds, were overlooked.

The three main peoples of Yugoslavia were the Serbs, Croats, and Bosniaks. Although all three groups shared a language that was virtually the same outside of regional differences, they had very different religious backgrounds. The Serbs are Orthodox Christians, use the Cyrillic alphabet, and consider themselves closely related to the Russians. The Croats are Roman Catholics, use the Latin alphabet, and see themselves more as Western Europeans. The Bosniaks are Muslims who although see themselves as European, also feel connected to Turkey.

A lid was put on the simmering problems during the communist regime that ruled Yugoslavia, but when communism crumbled throughout eastern Europe, the old rivalries came out, eventually ending in mass civilian atrocities and the partition of Yugoslavia. For a time some experts were afraid that the war was going to spread, with some even saying things such as "only every other world war starts in the Balkans."

Thankfully for all of us, the situation in the Balkans had greatly receded, although the tension in the region is still high.

How Do We Study World War One?

Hopefully you've learned quite a bit about World War One and had at least a little fun in the process. The first thing you should've learned about World War One and what should come to mind first is just how complicated this war was, which is how it should be studied and taught in the future.

Hopefully this book has sparked enough interest in some of you to go further and study World War One through more books that are available and maybe even by examining some of the primary sources. The primary sources can be newspaper accounts from the period, which are available on microfilm and increasingly in digital form online. Reading newspaper articles from the period will give you a general sense of what people were feeling and many of the political opinions of the time.

Another type of primary source that you may find useful in future studies are letters, diaries, and other forms of correspondence written by and to people who lived during the war. You can find these type of documents at local history museums and societies, or possibly at your local public library. Also, look around your family's house, especially if you've lived in the same place for a few generations you may be surprised at what you find in the attic.

Above all, the important thing to remember when you study and/or teach World War One is that it didn't take place in a vacuum. The series of events that led to the war and those that happened in the few years after is almost important as the war itself. World War One shaped the trajectory of twentieth-century history, but the trajectory that sent the world into war in 1918 was shaped in the nineteenth century.

Just remember to keep an open mind and have fun while you study the past.

RANDOM FACTS

1. Prime Minister George was the final member of the Liberal Party to serve as Prime Minister of the United Kingdom. George negotiated a peace with the Irish Republican Army (IRA) that eventually led to the formation of the Irish Free State in 1922 .

2. The Versailles Treaty called for plebiscites to be held in various regions to determine what country they would join. In the region of Silesia (it was then in eastern Germany, today it is part of Poland), the vote was to determine if the locals wanted to be part of Germany or Poland. The 1921 plebiscite in Silesia resulted in 707,000 votes for Germany and 479,000 votes for Poland. The Allies thought that there was pro-German vote tampering and divided the region according to voting patterns, resulting in the majority of the industries and mines going to Poland.

3. The mandates in Africa and the Middle East were pretty straight forward, with the French and British being given control of most of those countries, but the situation in the Pacific was a little different. Japan was given control over a large part of the South Pacific, although most of the islands were small and uninhabited. Australia

took control of the island nation of Nauru and New Zealand ran things for a while in Western Samoa.

4. President Wilson received a Nobel Peace Prize in 1919 for promoting the idea of the League of Nations, but ironically the United States never joined. The majority Republican Senate was against provisions in the League's charter that would've prohibited the United States from unilaterally declaring war, so they blocked America's entry into the failed organization.

5. After Roosevelt was elected president, a second, smaller Bonus Army, led by different people, descended on Washington with the same demands. Roosevelt provided accommodations for the marchers at Fort Hunt, Virginia. The First Lady, Eleanor Roosevelt, would later visit the camp, which helped take away much of the hostilities among the marchers. One marcher said, "Hoover sent the army, Roosevelt sent his wife."

6. The Treaty of Saint-Germain-en-Laye and the Treaty of Trianon was written by the Allies and imposed on Austria. The treaties regulated the new borders of Austria and Hungary, which left them both landlocked.

7. Kemal Ataturk (1881-1938) became the first president of the Republic of Turkey on October 29,

1923. He served as an officer in the Ottoman Army during World War One and became a leader in the Turkish War of Independence (1919-1923) before becoming president.

8. Although a vocal critic of the Nazis, Ernst Jünger was left alone by the regime and in fact was courted for membership, which he refused. Jünger did, though, serve in the Germany army during World War Two as an officer.

9. The Allies' harsh treatment of Germany after World War One was justified by Clause 231 of the Treaty of Versailles, where Germany was forced to admit guilt for having started the war.

10. There were a number of factors that led to Germany's hyperinflation cycle in the early 1920s. Massive war debt, the Allies occupation of the productive Ruhr Valley, low output of food, combined with too much currency in circulation all contributed to driving prices up.

11. When Frank Buckles died, President Obama ordered flags at all government building to be flown at half-staff. Buckles was interred at the Arlington National Cemetery.

12. The Zionist movement was a Jewish interpretation of nationalism. Many Jews were actually against it and believed that they should instead assimilate into European culture.

Theodore Herzl (1860-1904), a Hungarian Jew, is usually credited as being the ideological founder of Zionism, but Zionism never would've been successful without organization and funding, which was often provided by wealthy European Jews such as Walter Rothschild.

13. Among the right-wing organizations involved in political violence in Germany after World War One were the Freikorps. The Freikorps were comprised of many World War One vets who thought their government abandoned them and most were vehemently opposed to the new government in Weimar.

14. Armistice Day didn't become a legal holiday until 1938. The holiday became Veterans Day in 1954, when President Eisenhower signed a bill that changed the name into law.

15. Do you remember that Bulgaria was one of the Central Powers? Its involvement in World War One ended on September 29, 1918 when its leaders signed the Armistice of Salonica. The Bulgarians suffered far less in their peace with the Allies than the Germans, Austrians, and Ottomans did. The Bulgarians had to relinquish land they took in Greece and Serbia and demobilize their military. They weren't occupied and didn't have to pay crippling reparations.

16. President Wilson's health deteriorated rapidly after and some say because of World War One. He suffered a stroke on October 2, 1919 that left him partially paralyzed and largely ineffective for the remainder of his second term.

17. The National World War I Museum and Memorial is located in Kansas City, Missouri. The museum has many unique features, including replica trenches.

18. The list of films about or taking place during World War One is considerably shorter than those concerning World War Two. One of the more recent World War One films that did well at the box office was the 2011 film *Warhorse*.

19. Most historians agree that Franklin Roosevelt's landslide presidential victory in 1932 over incumbent President Herbert Hoover was largely the result of the Great Depression and Hoover's inability or unwillingness to do anything about it, but historians also agree that his treatment of the Bonus Army played a role in his demise.

20. Mehmed VI became ruler of the Ottoman Empire only about three months before his country surrendered, on July 4, 1918. After being removed from the throne, Mehmed VI lived and died in Italy but was buried in Damascus in the mosque of his illustrious ancestor, Suleiman the Magnificent.

Test Yourself – Questions and Answers

1. What did France hope to accomplish with the Treaty of Versailles?

   a. Punish Germany
   b. Punish the Ottoman Empire
   c. Punish Austria-Hungary

2. What was the Bonus Army?

   a. German right-wing war vets involved in post-war political violence
   b. An extra branch of the service the U.S. added after the war
   c. American World War One vets who protested not being paid a war bonus

3. Which was not a provision of the Treaty of Versailles?

   a. Almost total disbarment of the German military
   b. German reparations for starting the war
   c. The partitioning of Germany into West Germany and East Germany

4. Which country was Yugoslavia originally a part of?

   a. Germany
   b. Austria-Hungary
   c. Ottoman Empire

5. Which of these men was the last living American World War One vet?

    a. Frank Buckles

    b. Ernst Jünger

    c. George Kennedy

Answers

1. a
2. c
3. c
4. b
5. a

DON'T FORGET YOUR FREE BOOKS

GET THEM FOR FREE ON
WWW.TRIVIABILL.COM

DON'T FORGET TO CHECK OUT THE WORLD WAR 2 TRIVIA BOOK

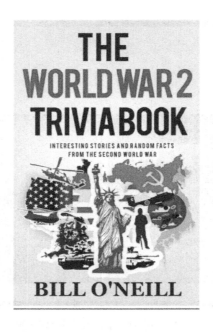

MORE BOOKS BY BILL O'NEILL

I hope you enjoyed this book and learned something new. Please feel free to check out some of my previous books on Amazon.